The **Ultimate** Knitted Tee

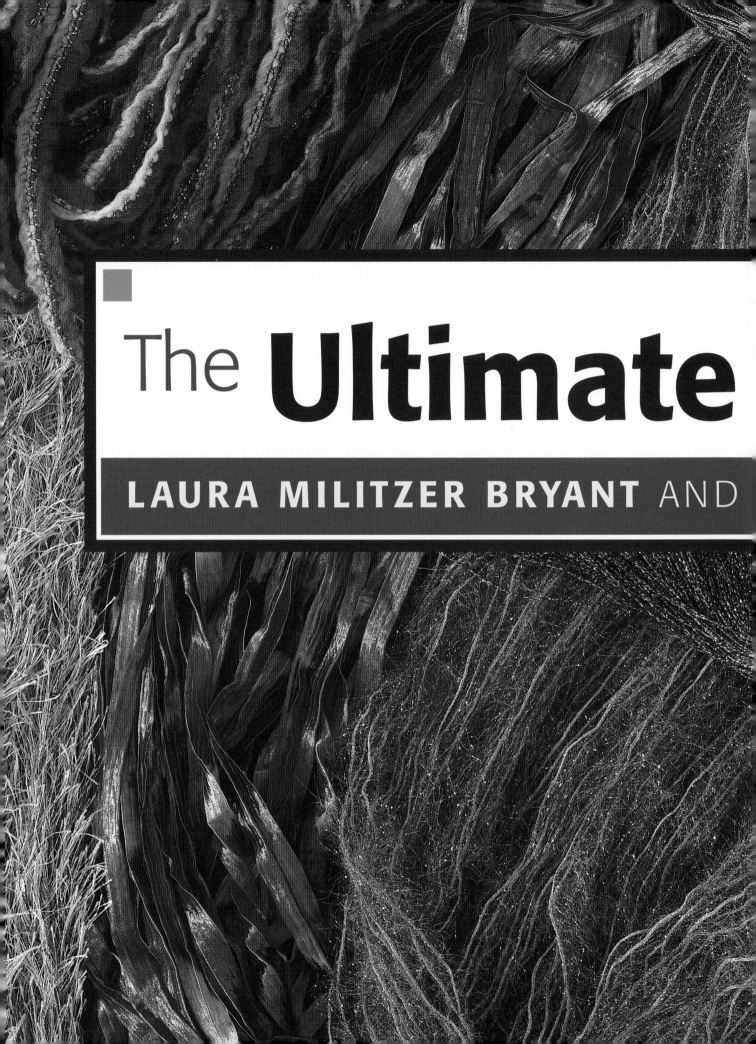

The **Ultimate**

LAURA MILITZER BRYANT AND

Knitted Tee

BARRY KLEIN

Martingale®
& COMPANY

Credits

President · *Nancy J. Martin*
CEO · *Daniel J. Martin*
Publisher · *Jane Hamada*
Editorial Director · *Mary V. Green*
Managing Editor · *Tina Cook*
Technical Editor · *Ursula Reikes*
Copy Editor · *Liz McGehee*
Design Director · *Stan Green*
Illustrator · *Robin Strobel*
Cover and Text Designer · *Trina Stahl*
Fashion Photographer · *John Hamel*
Photographer Assistant · *Troy Snyder*
Fashion Stylist · *Susan Huxley*
Studio Photographer · *Brent Kane*

The Ultimate Knitted Tee
© 2004 by Laura Militzer Bryant and Barry Klein

Martingale & Company
20205 144th Avenue NE
Woodinville, WA 98072-8478 USA
www.martingale-pub.com

Printed in China
09 08 07 06 05   8 7 6 5 4 3

Mission Statement

Dedicated to providing quality products and service to inspire creativity.

Library of Congress Cataloging-in-Publication Data

Bryant, Laura Militzer.
    The ultimate knitted tee / Laura Militzer Bryant and Barry Klein.
        p. cm.
    Includes bibliographical references.
    ISBN 1-56477-557-7
  1. Knitting—Patterns. 2. T-shirts. I. Klein, Barry. II. Title.
    TT825.B795 2004
    746.43'20432—dc22
                                    2004012858

Dedication

To the "Pretty Woman," who let the world know how cool knitting is.

To all of the celebrities who love to knit, who talk about it, and keep the craze going.

To the legion of new knitters—welcome to our world!

To the faithful knitters who have been with us for years—your passion inspires us.

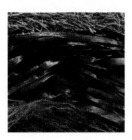

Acknowledgments

We would like to thank the many people who made this book possible:

The knitters without whose help there would not be any sweaters: Kay, Martha, Terry, Edna, Peggy, Fayla, and Jeanne;

The manufacturers of the beautiful yarns we used for the sweaters—thanks for rushing new samples and colors so that our books will always be fresh and new;

Kirstin Muench of Muench Yarns, and Stacy Charles and Diane Friedman of Tahki/Stacy Charles, who provided yarns for alternate choices;

Linda Cyr, who introduced Laura to garter boxes;

The retailers whose terrific stores showcase our products and the many other yarns available, and who provide assistance and education to knitters everywhere;

The knitters who are ever seeking to better their skills and make beautiful knitting music, who interact with us, and who serve as inspiration;

Our technical editor, Ursula Reikes, and the talented designers and photographers at Martingale;

The staffs of Prism and Trendsetter, who tend to business while we tend to books: Matt, Martha, Lillie, Diane, Zenaida, Di, Dragana, Rosa, Jennifer, and Debbie at Prism; Myrna, Heidi, Anita, Janet, Zuni, Ellie, Maggie, Jose, and Cesar at Trendsetter;

Our sales agents who are hard at work selling our yarns and books to stores; and

As always, our loving families who support our endeavors and give us the freedom to explore.

Contents

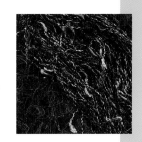

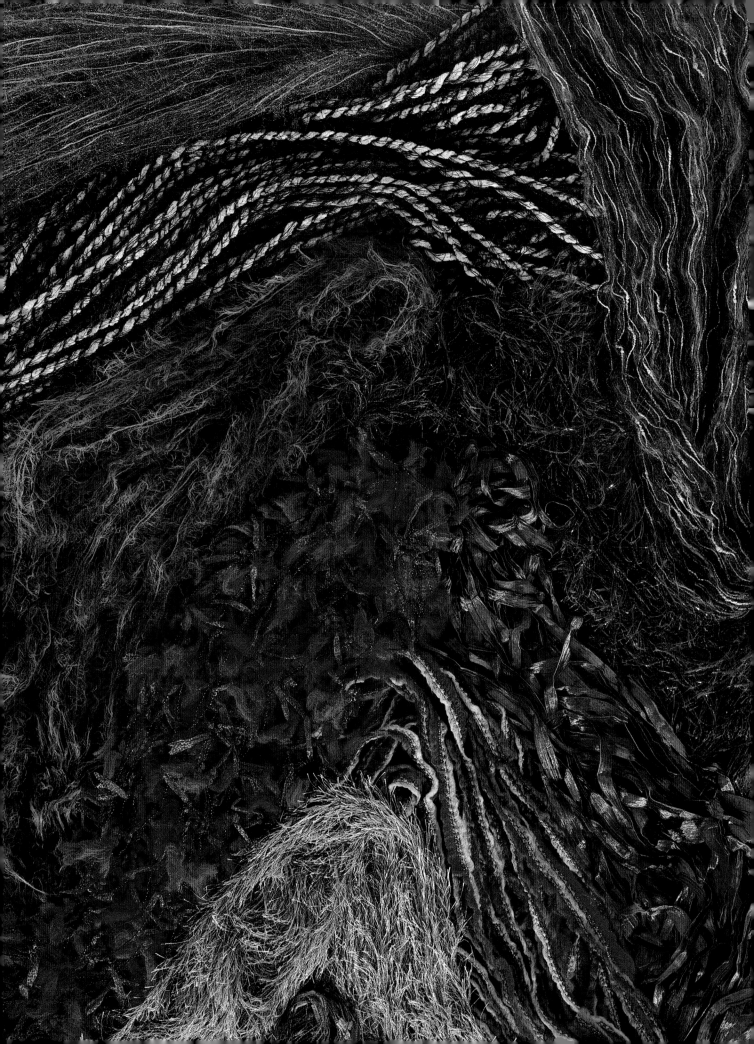

Introduction

What is the ultimate knitted tee? Comfy and easy fitting as a man's tee shirt, simple to knit, and quickly finished, tees are almost instant gratification. Once the body is done, you are practically there. Are you a new knitter? Are you looking for wonderful gifts to make? Are you ready to move on from scarves and try a garment? Are you an experienced knitter interested in mastering new techniques or experimenting with different and exciting yarns? Tees are the perfect answer. Our collection offers five approaches to knitting a tee, with each technique shown in four different themes.

Our five knitting styles take you on a tour through techniques and introduce newer knitters to skills they will need for each type of work. At the same time, experienced knitters will find enough challenge and creativity to entice them. The section "Bottoms Up!" explores the tradition of casting on at the bottom and working up to the shoulders. Different types of sleeves impart a sporty, tailored, or dressy look, and simple stripes and yarn changes are easily worked. "From the Top Down" takes us through the steps for almost seamless knitting, as we begin at the neck and work body, shoulders, and sleeves together, with a variety of neckline options and raglan detail. "A Sideways View", knitting from side to side, offers endless options for a slimming vertical line—who says you can't wear stripes? "Dynamite Diagonals" explores bias knitting that starts at one corner and increases both up and across with variations of color and pattern

work. "Pandora's Box" is a fun trip through a maze of garter stitch, where a square magically grows into a central motif, an entire body, or a decorative edge. All of these techniques are endlessly adaptable, and each chapter discusses which types of yarn are suitable, which styles best flatter your body type, and what new skills you'll learn as you complete the projects.

Yarn selection is always important to achieve the type of sweater that you want. We offer four distinct looks, from sporty to dressy with everything in between.

- Casual Comfort yarns are often simple and smooth, allowing for color and stitch-pattern work, with playful yet comfy textures used as accents.
- Workaday Wear yarns are a bit more refined. They may be smaller in gauge to fit under jackets and have an occasional hint of shine or texture. Details such as collars impart a more tailored look.
- Café Chic yarns ratchet up the novelty factor and include more texture, some sparkle, and a more playful approach.
- Glamour Girl yarns say it all. Exotic, sparkling, and dazzling fibers tell the story here.

Whatever your life style, body type, and knitting level, you are sure to find much to entice you in our parade of tees.

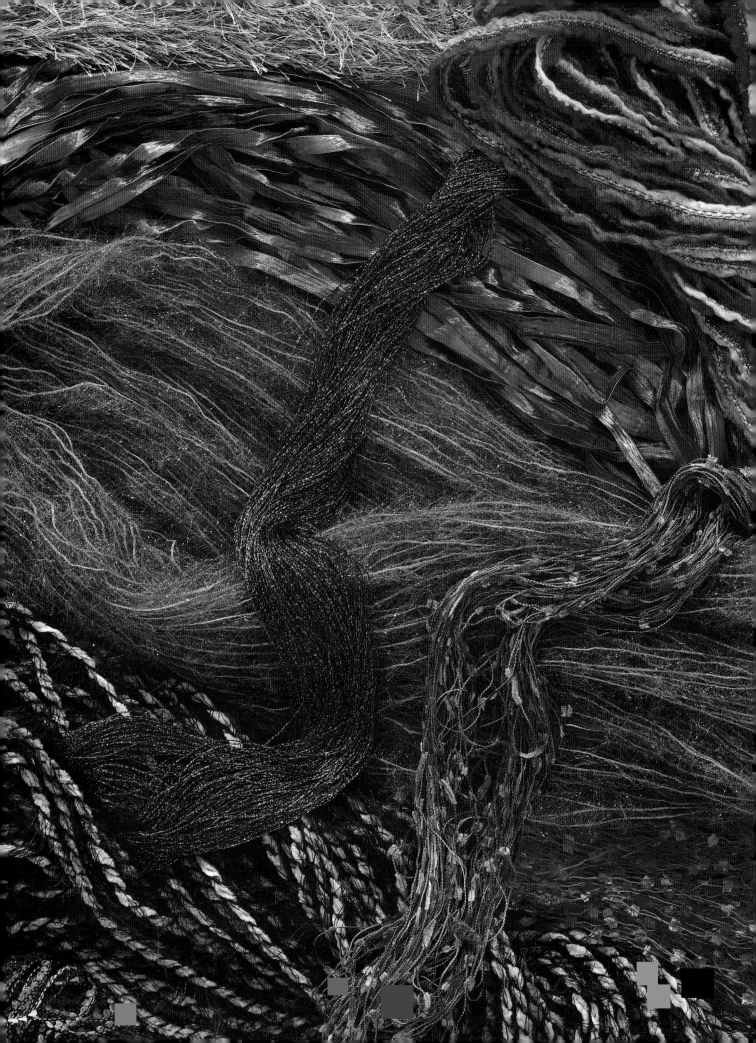

Getting Started

So, you know how to knit, you have made tons of great scarves, you are ready to tackle making a sweater—where do you begin? Most of the tees in this book are well suited to confident beginners, those who can cast on, knit, purl, and bind off. We know you have those skills, and we'll take you through the steps to build upon your knowledge and successfully make a garment. Specific techniques are discussed in every chapter, with skills being added as they are needed for the projects shown. Knitting is continually evolving, with new hints and ways of working, so even if you are an experienced knitter, we believe you will learn more. This chapter covers the basics that you need for any project you decide to make.

Gauge

The most important step in knitting successful garments is gauge—knowing what it is and how to adjust for it. When knitting scarves, gauge may not matter—a scarf doesn't need to be an exact finished measurement. A sweater, however, should fit the wearer appropriately: not too big, not too tight, sleeves the right length, neck opening the right size. You want to look and feel good in your new sweater and really show off your knitting skills. Nothing feels better than to have someone ask (with a smile of course): "Did you knit that yourself?" To achieve all of this, gauge is critical.

Think of making a gauge swatch as a great way to get to know your yarn. You can tell a lot about a yarn from your swatch: how it passes through your fingers, how you like working with the yarn itself, how the fabric feels after being knit, and even how the colors look together if you are using more than one. Often what one likes in the ball changes when the yarn is knit. Now is the time to discover any changes you might wish to make—not when you are halfway through the back!

The needle size needed to get a specific gauge is where knitters differ the most. Even if you are an experienced knitter who feels they are always "right on gauge," you need to make a swatch. There is no standard of gauge that designers can turn to, so you never know if the stated gauge was made by someone who is also "always right on" or by someone who isn't! Don't worry if you need to use a different needle size than the pattern says—remember it is just a suggested size. As we teach across the country, we constantly remind our knitters to always make a gauge swatch, even if you are using a yarn you have used before. Remember, if you don't make a swatch, you deserve what you get!

A good gauge swatch will be made over a minimum of 4" worth of stitches. All of the patterns in this book list the gauge at the beginning of the instructions and state the number of both stitches and rows that should equal 4". For example:

Gauge: 16 sts and 24 rows = 4" in St st on size 9 needles

This line of text contains much valuable information. It gives you a suggested needle size (9), it tells you what the pattern stitch is (stockinette stitch), and it tells you how many stitches to cast on for your swatch (16). Cast on 16 stitches and work pattern stitch for 24 rows. Take the swatch off the needle, lay it flat, and measure it. (The needle can distort the knitting.) You may have to lightly block the swatch to get it to lie flat. To block, hold a steam iron set on high over the wrong side of the swatch, but don't let the weight of the iron sit on the knitting. Give it a burst of steam, and gently tap the point and side of the iron on the edges. Lay a ruler on top of the swatch, flattening any residual curl. It should be a 4" square.

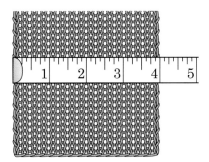

Stitch gauge is more important for fit, so let's concentrate on that. If your swatch is wider than 4", try again on a smaller needle. If it is narrower than 4", try again on a larger needle. When your swatch measures exactly 4" wide, the needle size is correct. You don't have to rip out the previous swatches; just put the swatch back on the needle and continue on a different-sized needle so that you can make a good comparison.

If you don't like the feel of the knitting after the needle change, then you may need to consider changing yarns. Just because you have gotten the right gauge does not mean the yarn is suitable for the project. You should consider things like drape, stiffness, body, and density of stitches.

One of Laura's favorite memories from her teen years involves making a vest from a weaving yarn that came on a cone. There was no label with suggestions for needle size or gauge, so she guessed. She knew she had to achieve the correct gauge to get the vest to fit, so she swatched until it was right, then happily knit and finished the vest, confident it would fit. Unfortunately, the yarn was knit on a needle far too small for it, and the completed vest was so stiff that it stood up on its own! This is a good lesson in checking your knitting after you get a few inches done—to see that the width measurement is correct (your tension can change as you work) and to make sure you like the feel of the knitted fabric.

To check the width, either work onto a circular needle so that you can spread the fabric out, or work half the stitches onto another long, straight needle. With a tape measure, follow along the cast-on edge as carefully as you can, and then compare the measurement to the diagram. If it isn't right, now is the time to change, not after you have knit the entire tee!

As for row gauge, this is the place that knitters differ the most. It doesn't mean your knitting is bad or incorrect; it may just be different than the sample knitter. You cannot change row gauge without affecting stitch gauge, and you really can't change how you knit. Trying to change gauge by consciously knitting tighter or looser will result in uneven knitting as you relax to your natural tension. If your swatch is not 4" high, but is 4" wide, this is still the needle you should use. You will find that you will use more yarn if your swatch is less than 4" high, because you are knitting more rows per inch. Or, you may use less yarn if your swatch is more than 4" high, because you are knitting fewer rows per inch. Over the course of a garment, a different row gauge can cause a variance of up to 20% in the yarn used than the amount called for in the pattern.

Row-gauge variation shouldn't affect the finished garment, because you are knitting to a measurement, not to the number of rows. It is handy to know if you differ from the pattern, though, so you can buy more yarn while it is available. Even if your row gauge is right on, check how much knitting is done after one ball has been used. You can now make a good guess about how much yarn you'll need for the entire garment. Measure how far you have gone. Compare this to the finished length measurement from the diagram at the end of the pattern. A quick bit of math will tell you how many more balls will be needed to finish the back. Divide the total length measurement (length of the garment along the side seam *or* along the bottom edge if knitting side to side) by the number of inches you have completed. The remainder is the number of balls needed for the back. The front will take the same, and two sleeves will take between one-half (for cap sleeves) and two-thirds (for short sleeves) of one body piece.

Even if you think you may need less yarn, it is still best to purchase the recommended quantity, as dye lots can change and it is better to have too much than not enough. Most stores will exchange yarn for store credit or new yarns within a specific time period. Be sure to check with the retail store you are buying from for their store's return policy. If you are unsure of your gauge, you may want to ask a sales person from your local store for help as well. The relationship you develop with the experienced knitters at your local yarn shop can be an invaluable resource.

What Size Am I?

The next important consideration is selecting size. There is no standard among designers and yarn companies as to what constitutes sizes such as Small, Medium, or Large, so while we have labeled each of our sweaters with the size, we also give a knitted bust measurement, and this is much more important than a size designation. Laura wears sweaters that vary from 38" to 44", depending on the style of the sweater and the yarn. This could be anything from a Medium to an Extra Large, depending on the designer.

Before you select a size, it is important to know your bust and hip measurements. Wrap a soft tape measure around your bust at the fullest point and again at the fullest part of your hip. You may wish to do this in front of a mirror to be sure that the tape going around your body is level. You may be laughing at this thought, but having the correct measurement truly is important. Also, no one will know but you. Or, have someone help you take measurements for accuracy. Swear them to secrecy and record the measurements for future reference.

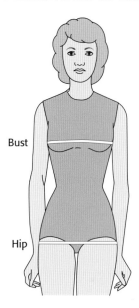

Additionally, you need to know how you like your clothes to fit. Pick a sweater from your wardrobe that has a fit you like. Lay the sweater flat and take a width and length measurement. Record these alongside your actual measurements. The difference between your actual measurements and the garment measurements is the ease. Like Laura, you may prefer different amounts of ease for different styles of sweaters.

Now you have the necessary information to pick a size. Consider the style of the tee: a casual fit will be more generous, while one meant to go under a jacket will be more fitted. Consider the thickness of the yarn: thinner yarns can be used to make larger garments if drape is desired, or smaller garments if they are fitted. Thick yarns can look too bulky if worked with too much ease, as they take on a size of their own, making you seem larger underneath. Look at the knitted measurements at the beginning of the pattern, and select the size with the width closest to your preference. Refer to your actual measurements, and make certain that your sweater is large enough to accommodate the larger of your measurements: hip or bust. If the sweater doesn't go over the fullest part of your hip, you needn't make it the full hip width, just big enough to sit nicely on the high part of the hip. Although knits fit wonderfully because of their natural give and stretch, you don't want the garment stretching over any part of your body.

Body Styles

It can also be useful to understand what type of body you have. All bodies are beautiful, but some sweater styles are more flattering than others for certain body types. We have used a symbol system in the introduction to each section.

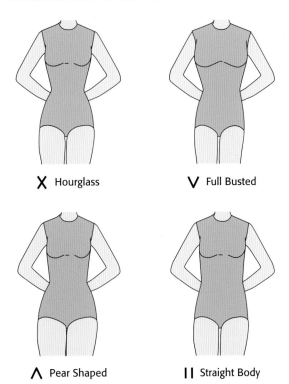

X Hourglass   V Full Busted

∧ Pear Shaped   ‖ Straight Body

X **Hourglass figure:** The bust and hip measurements are within a few inches of each other, with a narrower waist. The shoulders are usually fairly broad, and the entire impact is balanced and curvy. Long sweaters will make

you look boxy, as the hip and bust measurements are essentially the same. You can decrease stitches along the side edge as you move toward the waist, and increase back out to the bust width if you wish to give your narrow waist more definition. Shorter sweaters can begin with fewer stitches and increase toward the bust, since the tee will not go over the hips. Set-in sleeves give nice definition to broad shoulders.

V **Full busted, narrow hipped:** The bust is definitely larger than the hips, and the shoulders are generally broad. Cropped sweaters and those that end at the high hip will have a tendency to "flap in the breeze," with too much fabric around the bottom edge due to the width needed to fit the bust. A narrower bottom edge can be cast on, with stitches increased along the side edge to the wider bust. Longer sweaters will often drape enough that this isn't a problem. Set-in sleeves also give nice definition to the shoulders and keep excess fabric at the wider bust area from folding at the underarm, which can happen with drop shoulders.

∧ **Pear shaped:** The hips are larger than the bust and the shoulders are often narrow. Garment lengths will be more flattering if they are high hip, so the width doesn't need to be as large as the full hip. If a longer garment is desired, make sure the width is enough to accommodate the hips without stretching. Some of this extra width can be decreased along the side edge so that the bust will fit more naturally. Consider leaving the bottom portion of the side seams open for ease of wearing. Modified drop shoulders can extend the shoulder line visually, especially if a shoulder pad is used for definition.

‖ **Straight body:** Long, lean fashion models share this type with more ordinary mortals, whose bust and hips are basically the same measurement, with little waist definition.

Sweaters are the ideal garment for you. Straight shaping and most lengths will be flattering. If your shoulders are narrow, consider inserting small shoulder pads and make sure the shoulder line isn't sagging down your arm. If your shoulders are broad, set-in sleeves will give a more balanced look.

After each chapter discussion, we offer our suggestions for the visual impact of each style of knitting and which body types are best flattered by this style. The above ideas and methods of working hold true for all types of knitting, whether for yourself, a child, or the man in your life. As you work with other patterns to knit for yourself and loved ones, always make a gauge swatch and check it continuously, watch the yarn selection and quantity, select sizing by measurement and not by letter or name designation, and look at the body type you are knitting for to choose a flattering style. Successful knitting is just this easy!

Following Our Patterns

The beginning of each pattern gives all of the information needed to start your project.

Size: The designated labels in this section are arbitrary. The more important information follows.

Knitted bust measurement: This gives the actual finished circumference of the garment, at the fullest part, with ease included.

Materials: This is the amount of yarn it took us to make our model to the stated gauge and the needle size we used to get that gauge. If your row gauge is tighter, you'll need more yarn. If your row gauge is looser, you might have yarn left over. You may need a different needle size to obtain the gauge. If you make the sweater longer or shorter, you may need a different amount of yarn. If you select a pattern because you like the look of the sample, using the same yarn is important. In some cases, the yarn may be discontinued or your local yarn store may

not carry it, so if you have to substitute, the most important aspect to match is the stitch gauge. Once you have swatched the yarn, be sure that you like the look and feel of the knitted fabric, and be sure that the gauge matches.

Gauge: This is the stitches per inch you must get to make the garment fit as we designed it.

Stitch patterns: This provides the stitch patterns that are used in the garment. Follow the main pattern stitch for the gauge swatch, since different stitches can cause the yarn to work at a different gauge.

Back, front, sleeves: These are the actual directions for making each piece. We use abbreviations in writing patterns. You may look them up in the glossary, which is cross-referenced with the page where the technique is explained.

Finishing: This is how we suggest finishing the sweater, including the order of sewing seams and the type of edge finish. The chapter on finishing, "Wrapping It Up" on page 135, gives further information.

Diagrams: These are schematics of what the knitted pieces look like, complete with dimensions for each size. Check the diagrams before beginning to knit, and measure your knitting several times as you work to make sure you are keeping to those dimensions. When the knitting is finished, you can use the diagrams as guides if you decide to block your pieces (more on this in the finishing chapter).

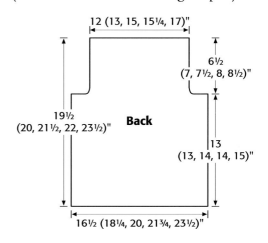

Yarn Substitutions

The yarns used in the model sweater are pictured, so you can see the kind of yarn each is and its thickness. At the end of each pattern, we offer some suggestions for alternate color combinations or yarns in a section titled "Changing the Look." This will help if you wish to substitute yarns. If you are using different yarns than the ones specified in the pattern, try to find yarns similar in thickness to the ones used. Notice that sometimes a flat ribbon yarn will look much thicker than a round yarn, when in reality it is only wider. The ribbon will fold in on itself to create the correct-sized strand. Figure the total yardage required by multiplying the yardage per skein by the total number of skeins specified in the pattern. Divide this figure by the yardage of the substitute yarn to figure how many skeins of the new yarn you'll need. Always round up, as it is much better to have some yarn left over than to run out.

Yarn Labels

Each manufacturer labels their yarns with important information. The name of the yarn, country of manufacture, fiber content, amount of yarn in the skein by both weight and yardage, the color number or name, dye-lot number, and suggested needle size and gauge can be found on most yarn labels. Here is what all of that means, and why it is important.

Color and dye lots: It is always a good idea to save a yarn label from each type of yarn you are using, in case you need more. If you do not know the dye lot, you cannot match it and there may be a line in your knitting when you change to a new lot. Sometimes the original dye lot is unavailable when more yarn is needed. In that case, before you knit all of the yarn in the old dye lot, begin alternating two rows of the new lot with the old. This will make the change much less noticeable.

Gauge and needle size: As we said in our prior discussion, knitters truly vary in their personal knitting style and tension, so needle size is always *only* a suggestion. Gauge is more important, as the manufacturer has determined at what gauge the yarn will look, feel, and behave the best. Although yarns can be knit at gauges other than specified, in general, try to stay within two stitches per 4" of a suggested gauge (one-half stitch per inch). An exception to this rule of thumb is when yarns are purposely knit on larger needles for a lacy, airy effect. If you are substituting yarns for a project, try to get a yarn with a similar suggested gauge.

Weight and yardage: This information allows you to figure out how much yarn is required if you are substituting. Find the yardage and number of skeins of the original yarn specified in the

prismyarn.com
ST. PETERSBURG, FL
PRISM

PRISM

by

CUSTOM
DYED
YARNS

Dry Cleaning Recommended
Biwa
Fiber Content: 100% Rayon
Color: *Mink*
Net Weight:1 oz Yardage: 68 yds.
#6 Needle Gauge 5 sts=1" Dye Lot #12193

pattern; for example, in Jukebox Jingle, the Medium requires 10 skeins of Prism Cotton Crepe at 75 yards per skein. Multiply 10 times 75 to get 750 yards total needed to make the sweater. If the substitute yarn gets the same gauge, divide the yardage total by the number of yards in the substitute. For example, to make this sweater out of Trendsetter Dolcino, which has approximately 100 yards per ball, divide 750 yards by 100 to get 7½ balls. Round up to 8 to be on the safe side, and you know how much yarn to buy. If the row gauge of the substitute yarn is smaller (more rows per 4"), you definitely will need more yarn; if the row gauge is larger (fewer rows per 4"), you might need less. Always keep an eye on the amount of yarn you have left. Don't wait until you are out before buying more. Once one or two skeins have been worked, you can measure how far they went, and by comparing to the diagram, make a best guess as to whether you need more. Now is the time to buy it so that you have the best chance of matching dye lots or incorporating any changes if necessary. The rest is up to you!

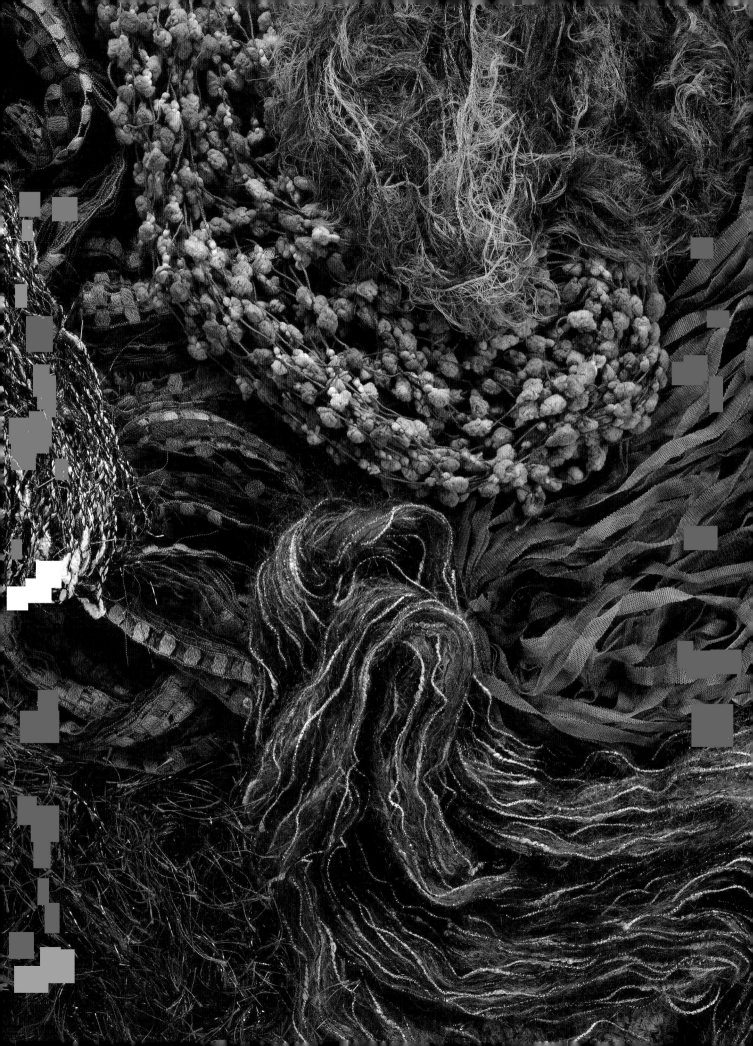

Bottoms Up!

The traditional way of constructing hand-knitted garments is from the bottom up on all pieces—front, back, and sleeves. While many variations exist, our simple tees have a minimum of shaping. The sleeves have caps that are shaped or straight across, or the sleeves are cast on and knit along with the body. The body may be worked up and over in one piece with no shoulder seam. You *must* match the stated gauge to achieve the correct fit when working from the bottom up.

Design possibilities are endless, with stripes, color blocks, cables, and other pattern stitches all fitting nicely into the scheme. While it is possible to knit the body up to the armholes on circular needles, we prefer seams, because they add definition and stability, and our patterns are written this way. To work circularly, simply cast on all of the stitches for both back and front and, being careful not to twist the cast-on row, join by working the first cast-on stitch and then each stitch around. When working circularly, all rows are right-side rows, so the pattern stitch must be adapted.

Design Options

The sky is the limit! Since this is traditional knitting, any pattern stitch and / or color work except stripes will easily adapt to these tees. Stripes will have a strong horizontal direction and may be better worked in another style unless the width of the stripes varies, the stripes are narrow, or they are used as accents instead of an allover pattern.

Yarn Suggestions

Anything goes here. Color work and intricate stitch patterns will show more in smooth, plain yarns. Simple stockinette and garter stitches show textured yarns to their best advantage. Alternating textured with smooth yarns is a great way to showcase novelty yarns, as is alternating stockinette and garter stitches.

Fit Tips

Bottoms-up sweaters offer the most flexibility for custom fit. Although all of the sweaters in this book have straight side edges, bottoms-up sweaters can easily be tapered at the side seams. The shoulder width and armhole type are most easily adjusted in this type of knitting as well. Any of these adjustments are explained in detail in our book *A Knitter's Template* (Martingale & Company, 2003).

X **Generally flattering:** You can taper the side seams so that the garment is narrower at the waist, and then widen them out again at the bust to provide definition for your hourglass figure. If your shoulders are very broad, a set-in sleeve, such as in Dots and Dashes on page 25, will be most flattering. Bring the seam line in a bit narrower than your actual shoulder measurement to minimize the shoulders.

V **Generally flattering:** Consider tapering the body by casting on fewer stitches at the bottom edge and increasing to the larger bust measurement. This will keep the bottom from being too loose. Set-in sleeves should sit just inside the natural shoulder line while a modified drop, as in Oceans Away on page 29 and Garden Party on page 33, will sit slightly outside the natural shoulder line.

∧ **Generally flattering:** Consider tapering the body by casting on more stitches at the bottom edge and decreasing to a smaller bust measurement. This will keep excess fabric from building up under the arms. If your shoulders are narrow, make sure the shoulder line is brought in enough to sit properly on the body. Set-in sleeves, in particular, will look neater and more tailored if the line is inside the actual shoulder. Consider adding a shoulder pad for more definition and to broaden the upper body line.

|| **Generally flattering:** This is great for slightly oversized, boxy styling.

Techniques: Beyond Getting Started

Refer to the following instructions as needed to complete your garment.

Bar Increase (K1f& b)
Working on the knit side, knit the first stitch normally, but don't remove it from the needle. Knit the same stitch again, into the back of the loop, and then slip the stitch from the left needle (2 stitches created from 1 stitch).

Knit into the front of the next stitch.

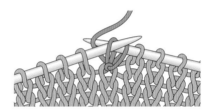

Knit into the back of the same stitch.

Decreases
There are 2 types of decreases and each slants in a different direction.

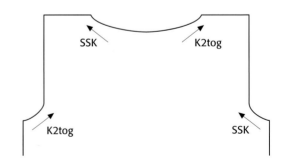

Left slanting decrease (SSK): To make a decrease that slants to the left (usually done at the right edge of your knitting, as in the beginning of a row or at the beginning of a shoulder area after binding off the center neck stitches), slip a stitch as if to knit, slip another stitch as if to knit (both stitches are on the right needle and twisted), slip both stitches together back to the left needle, and knit the two together through the back of both stitches.

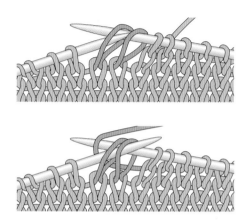

Right slanting decrease (K2tog): To make a decrease that slants to the right (usually done at the left edge of the knitting, as at the end of a row or at the end of a shoulder area before the bound-off neck stitches), simply knit 2 together by inserting the right needle into 2 stitches at one time and knitting them together, the same way that you would knit 1 stitch.

Cable Cast On

To cast on to existing knitting at the beginning of a row, make a stitch by inserting the right needle between the first and second stitches and wrapping the yarn around the needle. Pull the loop through to the front, and place this new stitch onto the left needle from the back side of the stitch. Repeat as often as necessary to achieve the new number of stitches specified in the pattern.

Circular Needles

If your sleeves are cast on and worked along with the body, as in Champagne and Caviar on page 37, there may be too many stitches to fit onto a straight needle. You can use a circular needle even if you are not knitting in the round. To transfer the stitches from your straight needle onto the circular needle, simply work the next row by using the circular needle. From now on, treat each end of the circular needle as separate needles, working back and forth. Notice that the weight of the knitting sits comfortably in your lap instead of dragging down the end of a long needle. If you are like Barry and don't enjoy working with circular needles, simply work with longer straight needles to accommodate the new stitches.

Stripes (Joining Yarn)

When working narrow stripes, as in Oceans Away on page 29, you can carry the extra yarn along the side edge, wrapping the new yarn around the old to keep it following along the selvage. When working wider stripes, such as in Garden Party on page 33, you can either carry along or cut and tie each yarn change, leaving a tail approximately 4" long to be buried in the side seam later. After seaming, thread the tail through a needle and run it through the seam ridge on the inside. We recommend burying the tail in the seam rather than in the body of the knitting because tails have a tendency to pop out of the actual knitting.

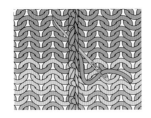

Picking Up Stitches for Knitted Bands

To finish a neck edge with a knitted band, as in Dots and Dashes on page 25, or a sleeve edge, as in Champagne and Caviar on page 37, you'll need to pick up stitches. Using a smaller needle than the one for the body, with the right side of the garment facing you, insert the needle between the first and second stitch on the edge, wrap yarn around needle and pull through—1 stitch picked up. Leaving this stitch on the needle, pick up the next stitch, and continue until all stitches have been picked up. The pattern will tell you how many stitches to pick up.

Divide the edge into 4 equal sections with safety pins or split-ring markers, and pick up one quarter of the stitches between each marker. When working around a neck edge, some stitches will be picked up directly into an existing stitch, such as along the back neck. Some patterns may call for this on the bottom band as well. Always spread the picked-up stitches out evenly across the area to be worked. If you find you have picked up too many stitches, simply work decreases that are evenly spaced across the first row.

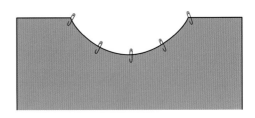

Casual Comfort: Dots and Dashes

Designed by Barry Klein

This is the true ultimate tee because it just looks and feels like a tee shirt. The yarn is a very wide ribbon, split in two shades of the same color that tweeds in the center. The design is created with a simple rib. Here's to the blue jean basic—stonewashed, faded, or dark. They all work with this sweater.

Stitch Patterns

Garter Ridge Stitch for Body
Row 1 (RS): Knit.
Row 2: *P9 (10, 11, 12, 13), K9 (10, 11, 12, 13);
     rep from *, end P9 (10, 11, 12, 13).
Rep rows 1 and 2.

Garter Ridge Stitch for Sleeves
Row 1 (RS): Knit.
Row 2: *P8 (9, 9, 9, 9), K8 (8, 9, 10, 10); rep
     from *, end P8 (9, 9, 9, 9).
Rep rows 1 and 2.

Back

- CO 45 (50, 55, 60, 65) sts. Work 3 rows in garter st.
- Work in garter ridge st for body to 13 (13, 14, 14, 15)" from beg or desired length to underarm.
- **Shape armholes:** BO 3 (3, 3, 4, 4) sts at beg of next 2 rows. Dec 1 st at each end EOR 3 (4, 4, 5, 5) times—33 (36, 41, 42, 47) sts.
- Cont in patt until armhole is 6½ (7, 7½, 8, 8½)". BO all sts in patt.

Front

- Work as for back until armhole is ½ (1, 1½, 1½, 2)".
- **Shape neck:** Work across 15 (18, 19, 21, 22) sts, then dec 1 (0, 1, 0, 1) st by working K2tog, join 2nd ball of yarn, and finish row—16 (18, 20, 21, 23) sts each side. Work each side at same time with separate skeins of yarn, dec 1 st at each neck edge every 3rd row 7 (7, 8, 8, 8) times—9 (11, 12, 13, 15) sts each side.
- Cont until front is same length as back and all neck shaping is completed.
- BO rem sts on each front, from armhole edge in.

Materials

- 6 (7, 8, 9, 10) skeins of Lane Borgosesia Jacquard (100 g, 60 yds), color 23
- Size 15 needles or size required to obtain gauge
- Size K crochet hook

Gauge:
11 sts and 14 rows = 4" in garter ridge stitch for body

Yarn shown at actual size.

Sleeves

- CO 40 (43, 45, 47, 47) sts. Work 3 rows in garter st.
- Work in garter ridge st for sleeves until sleeve is 5".
- **Shape cap:** BO 3 (3, 3, 4, 4) sts at beg of next 2 rows, dec 1 st at each end EOR until cap is 4 (4½, 5, 5½, 6)". BO 2 sts at beg of next 2 rows. BO rem sts.
- Rep for 2nd sleeve.

Finishing

- Sew shoulder seams.
- Set sleeves into body by centering cap to shoulder seam and working down each side.
- Sew rem underarm and side seams.
- Work 1 row of sc around neck edge, then work 1 row of sl-st crochet around neck edge to finish off.

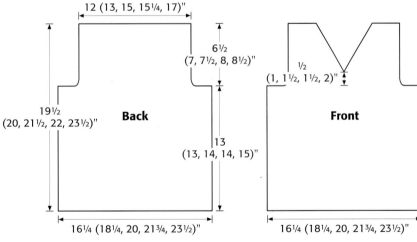

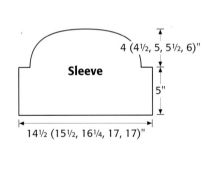

Changing the Look

Swatch A yarn: Trendsetter Genie (50 g, 35 yds), color 4080

Genie is an exciting yarn. The look will be similar to the model yarn, just more dramatic and a bit dressier.

To make the sweater from Genie, you'll need 12 (14, 16, 18, 20) skeins.

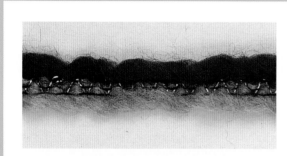

Yarn shown at actual size.

Swatch A

Swatch B yarn: Lane Borgosesia Merino Dodici (50 g, 70 yds), color 250

Merino Dodici is a 12-ply luxury wool that is a dream to knit. The style will stay simple, the stitches become more important, and the full-fashion details will play an important part in the finished look. To match the gauge, you need to work with 2 strands of yarn throughout.

To make this sweater from Merino Dodici, you'll need 10 (12, 14, 16, 18) skeins.

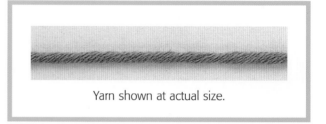

Yarn shown at actual size.

Swatch B

Workaday Wear: Oceans Away

Designed by Laura Bryant

Hot tropical colors distinguish this striped tee. The sequence is irregular, combining odd and even numbers of rows. This allows you to balance the colors visually: in this case, only a single stripe of fuchsia was needed in the sequence to add just the right amount of zip. To work the odd rows easily, knit the tee on circular needles, working back and forth. This way, you can slide the work to wherever the next color is waiting. Styled a bit slimmer and of smaller-gauge yarns than Dots and Dashes on page 25, this tee looks great under a jacket. And who says work clothes have to be boring? The faintest touch of glimmer adds an almost secret bit of fun to your day.

Stripe Pattern

5 rows with A

3 rows with B

2 rows with C

1 row with D

Note: To work odd rows of stripes easily, simply slide the work back and forth on the circular needle to wherever you need to be. Carry the extra yarns up either side edge, wherever they end up. Notice that when you slide the work to the other end, you will be working a second knit or purl row to keep the pattern in stockinette. Learn to recognize the knit side from the purl side: the knit side is smooth while the purl side is bumpy. Or, if you have trouble with this, place a safety pin at the beginning of the knit rows. If the safety pin is there, you will be knitting. If the safety pin is at the other end, you will be purling.

Back

- With size 3 needles and A, CO 100 (110, 120, 132, 144) sts. Work 6 rows in garter st.
- Change to size 5 needles and B, work stripe patt in St st to 11½ (12, 13, 14, 14½)" from beg.
- **Shape armholes:** BO 8 (10, 13, 14, 18) sts at beg of next 2 rows—84 (90, 94, 104, 108) sts.
- Cont in stripe patt to 19 (20, 21½, 23, 24)" from beg. BO all sts firmly.

Front

- Work as for back to 16½ (17½, 19, 20½, 21)" from beg.
- **Shape neck:** Work across 32 (34, 36, 40, 42) sts, join second ball of yarn and BO center 20 (22, 22, 24, 24) sts, finish row. Work each side separately, BO 3 sts at each neck edge once, BO 2 sts at each neck edge once, dec 1 st at each neck edge EOR 2 times—25 (27, 29, 33, 35) sts on each side.
- When same length as back, BO all sts firmly.

Sleeves

- With size 3 needles and A, CO 70 (74, 78, 82, 84) sts. Work 6 rows in garter st.
- Change to size 5 needles and B, work stripe patt in St st, inc 1 st at each edge every 3rd row 6 (7, 8, 8, 10) times—82 (88, 94, 98, 104) sts.
- Work until sleeve is 5 (5½, 6, 7, 7½)". BO all sts.
- Rep for 2nd sleeve.

Finishing

- Sew shoulder seams firmly.
- Set sleeves into armhole edge between bound-off sts of armhole on body.
- Sew side and sleeve seam, tacking edge of sleeve to bound-off sts of armhole.
- With A, work 1 rnd sc and 1 rnd rev sc around neck edge.

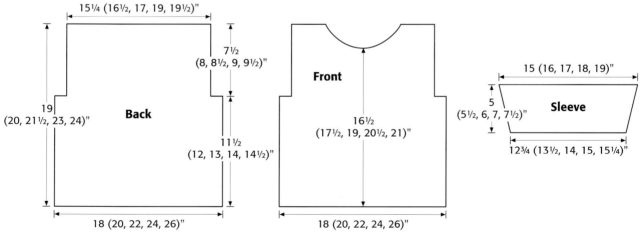

Changing the Look ▪ ▪ ▪ ▫

Swatch A yarn: Muench Bali (50 g, 150 yds), colors 82 (A), 63 (B), 85 (C), 2 (D)

Bali is a lovely, lightweight cotton-and-acrylic blend. Because the yarns are all solid, the stripes are much more pronounced than in the model.

To make the sweater from Bali, you'll need 4 (5, 6, 6, 7) skeins of A; 2 (2, 3, 3, 3) skeins of B; 1 (2, 2, 2, 3) skein of C; and 1 (1, 1, 1, 2) skein of D.

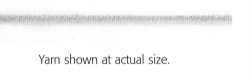

Yarn shown at actual size.

Swatch A

Swatch B yarn: Muench Tiffany (50 g, 120 yds), colors 103 (A), 7 (B), 1 (C), 4 (D)

Tiffany comes in tweedy solids and several multicolors. I chose one of the multicolored yarns for A. Because these are dyed by machine, the repeat of colors is much smaller, so the multicolored stripe becomes much more visually active, with little spots of color instead of stripes as in the model. Color D is very close to one of the colors in A, so it disappears in a single row and is barely distinguishable. The overall look is much less striped and more muted.

To make this sweater from Tiffany, you'll need 5 (6, 7, 8, 9) skeins of A; 3 (3, 3, 4, 4) skeins of B; 2 (2, 3, 3, 3) skeins of C; and 1 (1, 1, 2, 2) skein of D.

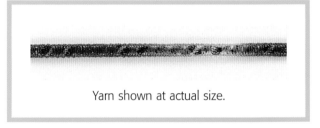

Yarn shown at actual size.

Swatch B

Café Chic: Garden Party

Designed by Laura Bryant

What soft, feminine fun! Who wouldn't love the extravagant loft and extreme softness of Duo, a fine eyelash nylon, paired with the interesting texture of Binario? Duo's lack of body (it tends to drape too much and lose its shape) is balanced by using 2 strands of Binario in alternating stripes. These garter bands not only provide visual punctuation but also add stability to the garment. Perfect for day to evening—dress it down with jeans; ratchet up the party factor with a broomstick skirt.

Size:

Small (Medium, Large, X-Large, XX-Large)

Knitted Bust Measurement:

36 (40, 44, 50, 54)"

Materials

- **MC** 4 (5, 5, 6, 7) skeins of Prism Duo (2 oz, 102 yds), color Garden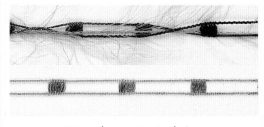
- **CC** 5 (6, 7, 8, 10) skeins of Trend-setter Binario (25 g, 82 yds), color 106 (work with 2 strands throughout)
- Size 10½ needles or size required to obtain gauge
- Size 9 needles
- Size H crochet hook

Gauge:

14 sts and 24 rows = 4" in stripe patt on size 10½ needles

Yarns shown at actual size.

Stripe Pattern

Rows 1–4: Work in garter st with 2 strands CC.
Rows 5–12: Work in St st with 1 strand MC.
Rep these 12 rows.

Note: Because Duo is very soft and malleable, it will "grow" substantially, becoming longer in length and narrower in width. We have compensated for the narrowing with more stitches; please measure your pieces for length while holding them upright to allow for downward stretch.

Back

- With size 9 needles and 2 strands of CC, CO 70 (78, 86, 94, 100) sts. Work 4 rows of CC.
- Change to size 10½ needles, cont in stripe patt to approx 14 (14, 14, 14, 16)", ending on garter-st rows.
- **Shape armholes:** BO 7 (9, 11, 11, 13) sts at beg of next 2 rows—56 (60, 64, 72, 74) sts.
- Cont as established to 8 (8, 9, 9, 10) stripe patt rep; approx 21 (21, 23, 23, 25)" long, measured holding upright to allow for downward stretch. BO all sts.

Front

- Work as for back to approx 18 (18, 20, 20, 22)", ending on garter-st rows.
- **Shape neck:** Work across 23 (25, 27, 30, 31) sts, join second ball of yarn and BO center 10 (10, 10, 12, 12) sts, finish row. Work each side separately, BO 3 sts at each neck edge once, BO 2 sts at each neck edge once, dec 1 st at each neck edge EOR once—17 (19, 21, 24, 25) sts on each side.
- When same length as back, BO all sts.

Sleeves

- With size 9 needles and 2 strands CC, CO 38 (40, 44, 48, 50) sts. Change to size 10½ needles, work stripe patt, inc 1 st at each edge every 4th row 8 times—54 (56, 60, 64, 66) sts.

- Work until sleeve has 3 (3, 4, 4, 4) stripe patt rep; approx 7½ (7½, 9½, 9½, 9½)" long.
- **Shape cap:** BO 4 sts at beg of next 12 rows. BO rem sts.
- Rep for 2nd sleeve.

Finishing

- Sew shoulder seams.
- Sew sleeves to armhole edges, between bound-off sts of armhole.
- Sew side and sleeve seams, tacking sleeve edge to bound-off sts of armhole.
- With 2 strands of CC, work 1 rnd sc and 1 rnd rev sc around neck edge.

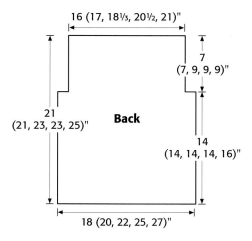

16 (17, 18⅓, 20½, 21)"

7 (7, 9, 9, 9)"

21 (21, 23, 23, 25)"

Back

14 (14, 14, 14, 16)"

18 (20, 22, 25, 27)"

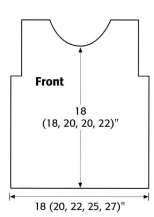

Front

18 (18, 20, 20, 22)"

18 (20, 22, 25, 27)"

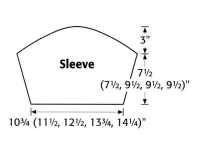

Sleeve

3"

7½ (7½, 9½, 9½, 9½)"

10¾ (11½, 12½, 13¾, 14¼)"

Changing the Look

Swatch A yarns: Muench Tessin (100 g, 110 yds), color 824 (MC), and Muench Mogador (100 g, 99 yds), color 135 (CC)

For a much more basic look, tweedy Tessin is alternated with smooth Mogador. The look is much flatter, with the stitches showing up distinctly. Since Mogador is thick on its own, it is worked singly. The finished tee will be much boxier, without the fluid drape of Duo, so make it less oversized and more closely fitting by dropping down one size.

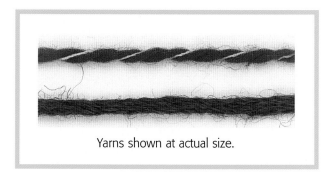

Yarns shown at actual size.

To make the sweater from these yarns, you'll need 4 (5, 5, 6, 7) skeins of Tessin and 2 (3, 3, 4, 4) skeins of Mogador.

Swatch A

Swatch B yarns: Trendsetter Coconut (50 g, 65 yds), color 126 (MC), and Trendsetter Dolcino (50 g, 100 yds), color 60 (CC)

Similar in feel to Duo, Coconut is a lofty, soft nylon. Its hairs tend to lie flatter than Duo's. Dolcino in a coordinating color is used singly and becomes a nice, contrasting accent. A tee made with these yarns will have much the same drape as the model. Notice that even though these 2 swatches were worked on the same-sized needle, and both measure to gauge over 4", the Tessin/Mogador swatch is marginally longer. Not to worry: either your tee is a bit longer, or you can eliminate some rows at the shoulder to make it the same length.

To make the sweater from these yarns, you'll need 6 (8, 8, 10, 11) skeins of Coconut and 2 (3, 3, 4, 4) skeins of Dolcino.

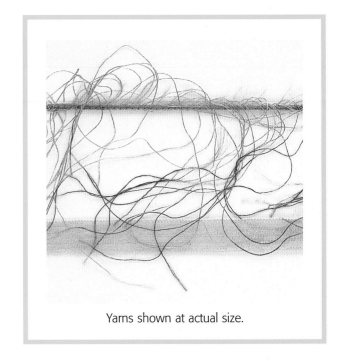

Yarns shown at actual size.

Swatch B

Glamour Girl: Champagne and Caviar

Designed by Barry Klein

There are times when you plan a design and it just doesn't work. This design had that problem. The original was worked in yarns that just didn't fit the style when it was finished. I showed it to Laura, looked in her eyes, and knew this boat was not going to float. Loving the design but not the yarns, I switched to new yarns, swatched them, and voilà—you have the richest of all rewards: champagne and caviar. The scarf was a last-minute addition and it plays two roles: a wonderful collar finish and the ultimate accessory that we love to make and wear. We drink a toast to the sweater; it's all glamour on this girl.

Front

Sweater is worked up the front, over the shoulders, and down the back in one piece.

- With size 13 needles and B, CO 41 (46, 51, 56, 61, 66) sts. Work 3 rows of garter st.
- Change to A, work in St st to 10 (10½, 11, 11½, 12, 12½)" from CO.
- **Shape sleeves:** Cont in St st, inc 1 st at each end EOR 3 times—47 (52, 57, 62, 67, 72) sts. Cable CO 4 (4, 4, 5, 5, 5) sts at beg of next 4 rows.
- Cont on 63 (68, 73, 82, 87, 92) sts in stripe patt as follows: *4 rows with B in garter st, 4 rows with A in St st. Rep from * to 2½ (3, 3½, 4, 4½, 5)" from beg of sleeve CO.
- **Shape neck:** Work across 23 (25, 28, 32, 35, 37) sts, join second skein of yarn and BO center 17 (18, 17, 18, 17, 18) sts, finish row. Work both sides at same time with separate skeins of yarn, cont in stripe patt until 5 (5½, 6, 6½, 7, 7½)" from beg of sleeve CO. Mark beg and end of row. Front is now completed.

Back

- **Shape neck:** Cont in patt, inc 1 st at each neck edge on next row, and then EOR 2 more times. Cable CO 2 sts at beg of each neck edge once. Cable CO 7 (8, 7, 8, 7, 8) sts at neck edge, work across, joining 2 sides into 1 piece again—63 (68, 73, 82, 87, 92) sts.
- Cont in stripe patt to 5 (5½, 6, 6½, 7, 7½)" from shoulder marker.
- **Shape sleeves:** Change to A only and BO 4 (4, 4, 5, 5, 5) sts at beg of next 4 rows, dec 1 st at each end EOR 3 times—41 (46, 51, 56, 61, 66) sts.
- Cont to 10 (10½, 11, 11½, 12, 12½)" from last dec.
- Change to B and work garter st for 3 rows. BO on next row.

Finishing

- With size 13 needles and B, PU 36 (38, 40, 42, 44, 46) sts along sleeve edge. Work in garter st for 3 rows. BO on next row. Rep for other sleeve edge.
- Sew underarm and side seams.
- With A, work 1 row of sc around neck edge.

Scarf

- With size 15 needles and A, CO 16 sts. Knit back.
- Work in garter st and stripe patt as follows: 2 rows with B, 2 rows with A.
- Work until scarf is 48" long. BO at end of next A stripe.
- Cut extra yarn and fringe beg and end of scarf as desired.
- Fold scarf in half lengthwise and join to center of back neck. Sew scarf around back neck edge and 1" down on each front. Allow scarf to hug neck and hang or fold, roll, and toss one end over the other. Scarf can also be left unattached and used as an accessory with other outfits.

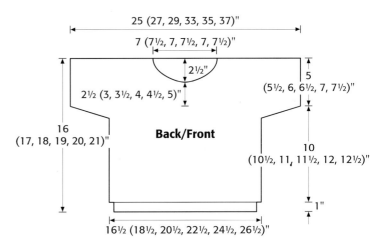

Changing the Look

Swatch A yarns: Trendsetter Blossom (50 g, 90 yds), color 11, and Trendsetter Aquarius (50 g, 95 yds), color 821

The original design is very dressy, flamboyant, and luxurious. Since I love the design but not everyone needs that "special" top, these 2 yarns will make a wonderful tee that will take you through the entire day. They will also make a wonderful scarf, whether attached to the sweater or worn separately.

To make the sweater from these yarns, you'll need 6 (7, 7, 8, 8, 9) skeins of Blossom and 2 (3, 3, 3, 3, 3) skeins of Aquarius.

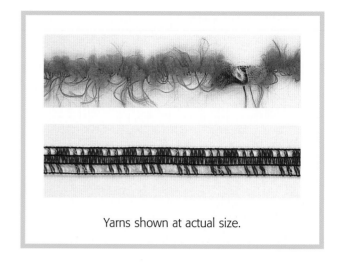

Yarns shown at actual size.

Swatch A

Swatch B yarns: Trendsetter Checkmate (50 g, 70 yds), color 1039, and Trendsetter Crisantemo (50 g, 55 yds), color 3

By using Checkmate as the body yarn, you will have a sweater that fits all moments of your life, from casual to dressy. This ribbon alternates between sections of shiny checkerboards and matte ribbon to bring color and texture to the body. For some extra pizzazz, the Crisantemo, with its wild lashes, adds some frill and fun to the finished sweater. Again, these 2 yarns will make a fantastic scarf, attached or left free to enjoy alone.

To make the sweater from these yarns, you'll need 8 (9, 9, 11, 11, 12) skeins of Checkmate and 4 (5, 5, 5, 6, 6) skeins of Crisantemo.

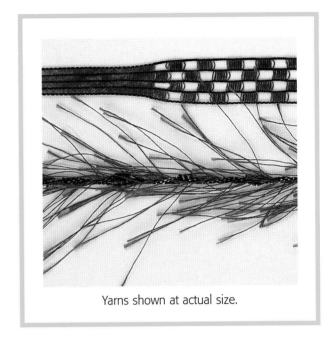

Yarns shown at actual size.

Swatch B

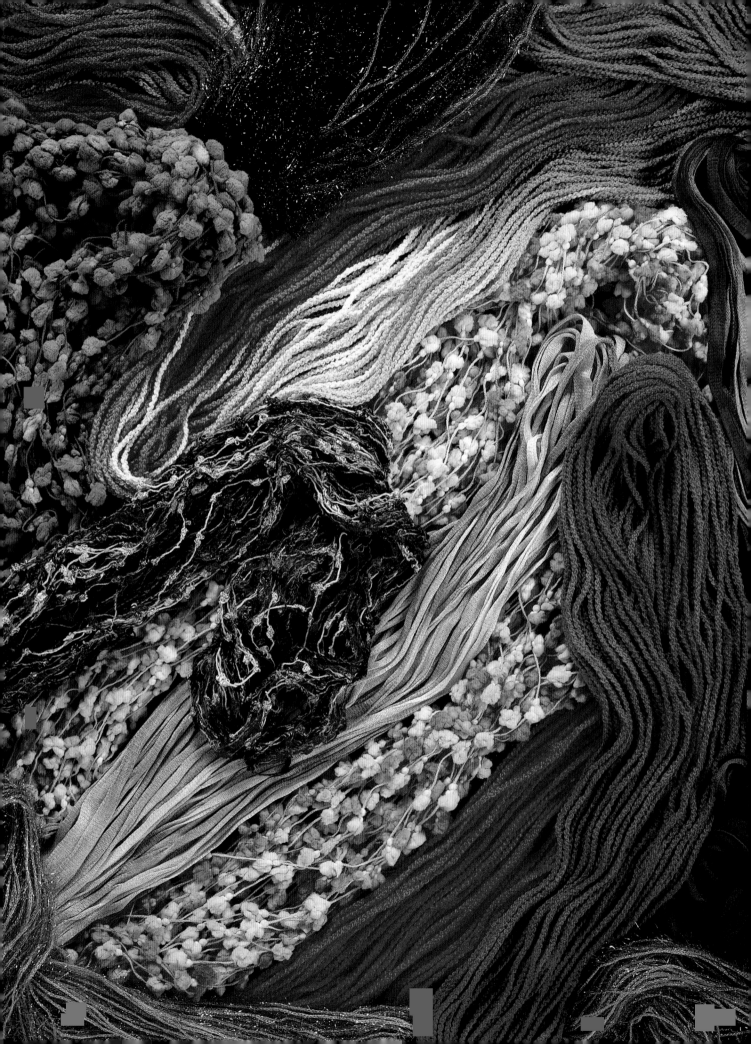

From the Top Down

It all starts with a few stitches at the neckline and grows like magic from there. Front, back, and sleeves take shape before your very eyes as all pieces are knitted seamlessly and at once in raglan style. While it might seem a bit confusing at first, once you have mastered the concept and the technique, you'll love it. Since all pieces are made at the same time, matching stripes or patterns is also seamless. When designing your own sweater, select a pattern stitch that is easy to increase and contains a small-enough repeat to start on the few stitches we begin with at the neck.

The first few inches are worked back and forth to provide proper neck shaping (lower in front). Once the neck shaping is complete, the stitches are joined and worked in the round while the raglan increases continue and the body and sleeves grow. One benefit of knitting a sweater from the neck down is that you can try it on as you work. Increases can become more frequent if you require more stitches at a faster rate, or they can be spaced out more slowly to keep the body and sleeves from getting too full. The most important measurement to keep track of is the armhole depth, which is measured as the depth of the raglan. As the raglan continues to grow in length, the body and sleeve width will increase as well. Be sure to try on the garment every few inches and look in the mirror to check the fit. You may have to split your stitches between two circular needles in order to spread the knitting around your body and keep from losing stitches. We can't stress enough that it is easy for this style of knitting to get too full in both body and sleeve. Since you can try the sweater on as you work, you have total control over achieving the perfect fit. Once the armhole is the correct depth and the sleeve and body are the desired width, the sleeve stitches are placed on holders, underarm stitches are cast on, and the body is joined for circular knitting—no seams! Later, you return to the sleeves, which can be knit circularly or worked back and

forth and seamed. Add a finish to the neckline and the sweater is done!

Design Options

One of the most interesting design elements is the type of increase used in the raglan shaping. Standard bar increases (see page 22) become more important when separated by several stitches, providing a flat band of definition between sleeves and body, as in Jukebox Jingle on page 47. These stitches can be worked in a different stitch pattern, such as garter, seed, or cable, as in Cablegram on page 51. When selecting a decorative stitch for this purpose, make sure that the row gauge is compatible with the body-pattern row gauge, or the shaping will not work.

A less visible increase is a blind increase (see page 45). Another decorative increase is a yarn over (see page 45), which makes a stitch and leaves an eyelet hole at the same time, as in Luminary on page 59. This works well in a small-repeat pattern stitch where it is easier to put the stitch into the pattern on subsequent rows. The textured yarns of Luminary tend to hide the eyelets, but it is a lovely feminine detail when using a classic yarn, such as a smooth, summery cotton.

Yarn Suggestions

Top-down knitting is great for most yarns. However, very thick yarns (less than three stitches per inch) can be problematic since it is difficult to achieve the correct rate of increase. Heavy yarns may stretch in the shoulder and neck area as there are no seams to add stability, but the fact that these are short or cap-sleeved tees makes this less of a problem. Since the number of stitches is constantly changing, consider any patterning or striping that may happen with multicolored yarns, where this will fall on the body, and how the color change will affect the overall look. Short color repeats will work up with a mottled look, and yarns with long color repeats will create stripes that become narrower as the stitch count increases.

Fit Tips

This is an excellent style for anyone with sloped shoulders and not a great choice for someone with very square shoulders, because there is slope built into the sweater naturally. Striped patterns in particular are flattering to broad shoulders because the stripes move up and over at the shoulder instead of straight across.

X **Generally flattering:** Keep in mind that this style of sweater tends to be more boxy and full so your waistline will not be highlighted. As you become more advanced, you can place markers where the side seams would be and work decreases there to shape the waist, and then increase again toward the hips.

V **Not always the most flattering:** There tends to be more fabric around the bust, which may make the bottom half too full. Stitches could be decreased as the body is worked down, or a tighter bottom band can be worked to pull the bottom in.

∧ **Very flattering:** The sweater is more fitted around the shoulders. By making the armhole deeper, the body becomes wider as it continues down, while the shoulders stay neat. For really full hips, a shorter, high-hip length is more desirable since the width won't have to accommodate the fullest part of the body. Or, continue to increase after the body is joined to get a larger bottom edge. You may opt to work the last few inches back and forth with a slit at the sides.

II **Generally flattering:** Be sure to watch the armhole depth carefully so that the sweater fits more closely and doesn't get too boxy.

Techniques: Beyond Getting Started

Refer to the following instructions as needed to complete your garment.

Yarn-Over Increase

This increase is worked on the knit side. Complete the stitch before the yarn over, bring the yarn forward between the 2 needles, lay it over the right needle (yarn over made), then work the next stitch as established.

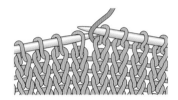

Blind Increase

This increase is made by picking up the thread that runs between the stitch just worked and the stitch marker and putting it on the left needle from the front. Using the point of the right needle, knit the new stitch from the back (so that it twists) to avoid making a hole.

Knitting in the Round

Circular needles are thin flexible wires or cables with short needle ends that correspond to straight needles in size. Circular needles are used when there are too many stitches to fit comfortably on a straight needle and for seamless knitting in the round. To work in the round, join the knitting, being careful not to twist it (you will create a Möbius strip if you do), place a marker so you know where each round begins, and work continuously. Stockinette stitch is the easiest to do, since every round will be knit. If you wish to work garter stitch, you must alternate 1 round of knit and 1 round of purl.

Cables

Cables are small numbers of stitches that are twisted over one another to create a braid on the surface of the knitting. Cables are usually knit stitches that are separated from the body of the work by purl stitches on either side. They are easy to master, even for beginners.

- On the row you are to work the cable, work to the cable stitches.
- Slip the required stitches to a cable needle (a short needle with a curve that will hold the stitches while you work the cable).
- Hold in front or back of the work as directed by the pattern.
- Knit the next stitches on the needle.
- Slip the stitches from the cable needle back to the left needle, and knit these stitches.

Always slip the stitches as if to purl to keep them from getting twisted.

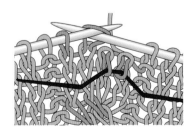

Stitch Holders

Stitch holders are essentially large safety pins. They securely hold stitches that you are not currently working on for future use. To transfer stitches to a holder, open the holder and, using the open end as a needle, enter each stitch as if to purl and slip it onto the holder.

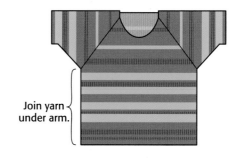

Join yarn under arm.

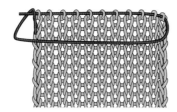

Stripes in the Round

When stripes are worked in the round, as in Jukebox Jingle on page 47, there is a jump when a new color is started. We have found that the best way to work with this is to hide the jump in an inconspicuous place, such as moving the join to the back raglan shaping or to the side, under the arm. Since there is no seam to hide the ends in, the ends can be woven into the back of the stitches as you work them.

Better yet, once the body is begun, split the stitches at the underarm of one side and work back and forth. You will have one seam to sew, but you can sew it invisibly so that the stripes match exactly, with no jog where the colors change.

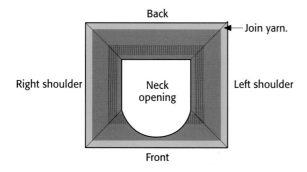

Back

Join yarn.

Right shoulder

Neck opening

Left shoulder

Front

Casual Comfort: Jukebox Jingle

Designed by Laura Bryant

Like the flashing neon lights of a '60s jukebox, this fun, striped tee dances. It's hard to keep your toes from tapping and definitely hard not to smile with all of that color going on. Pure saturated solids are punctuated with the kinetic energy of a full spectrum multicolor. Mix up the stripes—the work is more interesting if the stripes aren't regular. A crisp-bodied cotton crepe gives structure to the tee, yet stays cool enough for comfort. This sweater is great paired with jeans or jewel-toned slacks.

About stripes: You may use as many or as few colors as you wish. We used four solids and one hand-dyed multicolor. The stripes are worked in any repeat of the following numbers: 1, 2, 3, or 5 rows. For more interest, change each yarn at random and mix up the row counts for each color at random. Because you are working in the round, the odd number of rows does not increase the difficulty of your knitting. The stitches are well defined and easy to count, but if you have trouble, keep a row counter going to keep track of the increases. Each yarn will be cut when changing colors. Once you cast on the neck stitches and join for circular work, shift the changing of colors to the beginning of the left back shoulder increase (this will show the least). Once you have joined the complete body under the sleeves, you can continue to change the yarns at this point or you can shift the change to under one arm, as if it were a side seam, where it will show less. If you wish to have the cleanest look, with no "jump" when the colors change, work the body back and forth with the stitches broken at one underarm, and seam this later, matching the stripes exactly.

Body

- With size 8 needles and any color, CO 40 (44, 46, 50, 52) sts.
- Purl back and place markers (pm): P1 front, pm, P2 raglan, pm, P5 (6, 6, 7, 8) shoulder/sleeve, pm, P2 raglan, pm, P20 (22, 24, 26, 26) back neck, pm, P2 raglan, pm, P5 (6, 6, 7, 8) shoulder/sleeve, pm, P2 raglan, pm, P1 front. Turn work.
- Inc and slip markers as follows: K1f&b, slip marker, K2, slip marker, K1f&b, knit to 1 st before next marker, K1f&b, slip marker, K2, slip marker, K1f&b, knit to 1 st before next marker, K1f&b, slip marker, K2, slip marker, K1f&b, knit to 1 st before next marker, K1f&b, slip marker, K2, slip marker, K1f&b—8 inc made. (You should always

have 2 sts between each pair of markers; visually, there will be 3 sts lined up at each increase point.)

- Cont in St st, inc as established EOR and AT SAME TIME inc 1 st at each neck edge every 4th row 2 times, then EOR 3 times.

- After 16 rows, cable CO the number of sts necessary to make front sts equal to back sts. Join and cont in this color for at least 1 more row. Cut the yarn.

- Attach new yarn at beg of left back shoulder, between the markers, by slipping each st as if to purl to right needle until you reach the left back. This will move the color change to an inconspicuous spot.

- Cont in rnd, in stripe patt, work inc as established, until there are 66 (72, 76, 82, 86) sts between markers on back. The work should be approx 7¾ (8, 8½, 9, 9½)" from original CO. This is depth of armhole. If you are within ½" of the measurement for your size, don't worry about it. If your armhole has gotten too deep, rip back as needed, and add the extra sts to the number CO at underarm. If armhole is not deep enough, work a few more inc rows and take extra sts away from underarm CO.

- Place sleeve sts on holders as follows: work across back sts, drop marker, K1, sl next st to holder, drop marker, sl sleeve sts to holder, drop marker, sl 1 st to holder, cable CO 6 (8, 10, 10, 14) sts for underarm, K1, drop marker, work across front, drop marker, K1, sl next st to new holder, drop marker, sl sleeve sts to holder, drop marker, sl 1 st to holder, cable CO 6 (8, 10, 10, 14) sts for underarm, K1, drop marker—144 (160, 172, 184, 200) total sts.

- Move yarn change to middle of one underarm (don't worry about an extra half row on part of the body). Work body in rnd or back and forth for 10½ (11, 11½, 12, 12½)".

- With size 6 needles, work in K1, P1 rib for 1". BO all sts loosely in patt.

Sleeves

- With size 8 needles, place one set of sleeve sts onto needle, CO 3 (4, 5, 5, 7) sts, work across sleeve sts, CO 3 (4, 5, 5, 7) sts at beg of next row.

- Work stripe patt as for body, dec 1 st at each edge every 3rd row 9 times.

- Cont until sleeve is 4½ (5, 5½, 6, 6½)" from CO row.

- With size 6 needles, work in K1, P1 rib for 1". BO all sts in patt.

- Rep for 2nd sleeve.

Finishing

- Sew any seams.

- With size 6 needles and any color, PU 60 (62, 64, 64, 66) sts around neck edge. Work in K1, P1 rib for 1½", using random stripes as for body.

- BO in patt loosely enough to allow for stretch over head, but firmly enough that edge lies flat.

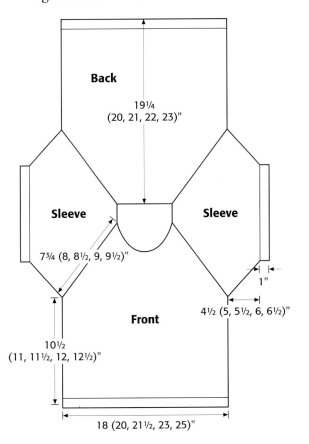

Back

19¼ (20, 21, 22, 23)"

Sleeve   Sleeve

7¾ (8, 8½, 9, 9½)"

1"

4½ (5, 5½, 6, 6½)"

Front

10½ (11, 11½, 12, 12½)"

18 (20, 21½, 23, 25)"

Changing the Look

Swatch A yarns: Prism ¼" Rayon Ribbon (2½ oz, 95 yds), color Periwinkle, and Prism Luna (1 oz, 58 yds), color Arroyo

Rayon ribbon lends a crisp, tailored look to this swatch. A coordinating color of Luna is selected and worked every 7th and 8th rows in garter stitch as an accent. You can figure out how much of each yarn you need because there is an 8-row repeat, and 2 rows of every 8, or 25%, are worked in the accent yarn. So, for the total yardage, 25% would be the accent and 75% would be the main color.

To make the sweater with these yarns in the stripe patt, as in the swatch, you'll need 5 (6, 7, 7, 8) skeins of Ribbon and 3 (3, 3, 3, 4) skeins of Luna.

Swatch B yarn: Trendsetter's Dolcino (50 g, 99 yds), colors 105, 108, 8, 106

Dolcino gives the same kind of stitch definition as the Cotton Crepe we used in the model sweater, but with a silkier hand and a more refined look. Rank the colors you select according to brightness or impact, and use more of the muted ones while throwing in some zingers for spice!

To make the sweater with Dolcino, you'll need a total of 7 (8, 9, 9, 10) skeins.

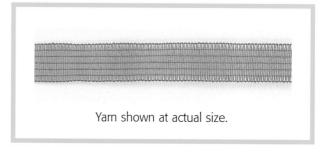

Yarn shown at actual size.

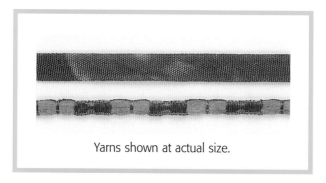

Yarns shown at actual size.

Swatch B

Swatch A

Workaday Wear: Cablegram

Designed by Barry Klein

One of the intriguing aspects of knitting from the top down is figuring out what you can do with stitch patterns in and around the raglan decrease—the possibilities are endless. I selected Dune yarn for this workaday tee because I thought that the cabled rib in the raglan decrease would add some texture. Since the yarn is space dyed, the colors in the yarn play a big part in the circular flow created. A solid-colored texture at the edge of every piece adds an interesting touch and allows you to wear this wonderful sweater with any color outfit. Ready to dress for work?

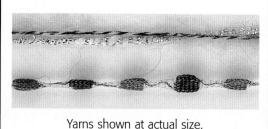

Stitch Patterns

Rib Pattern

Row 1 (RS): *K2, P2; rep from *.
Row 2: Knit the knit sts and purl the purl sts.
Rep row 2.

Cable Pattern

Rows 1, 5, and 7 (RS): P1, K6, P1.
Rows 2, 4, 6, and 8: K1, P6, K1.
Row 3: P1, sl 3 sts to cn and hold in back, K3, K3 from cn, P1.

Cable Rib Pattern

Rows 1, 5, and 7 (RS): *P2, K2, P2, K6; rep from *.
Rows 2, 4, 6, and 8: Knit the knit sts and purl the purl sts.
Row 3: *P2, K2, P2, sl 3 to cn and hold in back, K3, K3 from cn; rep from *.

Body

- With size 9 needles and A, CO 70 (70, 76, 76, 78) sts as follows: 1 st front neck, 1 st front body, pm, 8 sts cable patt raglan, pm, 6 (6, 8, 8, 8) sts shoulder/sleeve, pm, 8 sts cable patt raglan, pm, 22 (22, 24, 24, 26) sts back neck, pm, 8 sts cable patt raglan, pm, 6 (6, 8, 8, 8) sts shoulder/sleeve, pm, 8 sts cable patt raglan, pm, 1 st front, 1 st front neck.
- Work body sts in St st and raglan sts in cable patt, inc (K1f&b) in st before first and after second marker on each side of raglan cable patt EOR until raglan is 7 (8, 9, 10, 10½)". AT SAME TIME shape neck, inc (K1f&b) at neck edge every fourth row 4 times. Cable CO 2 sts at beg next 2 rows. Cable CO on number of sts as necessary to make front sts equal to back sts. Join work.
- With RS facing, knit every rnd in body sts and work 8 sts in raglan sections, following

row 1 of cable patt on every rnd, except twist cable following row 3 of cable patt.

- Work in rnd until raglan is 7 (8, 9, 10, 10½)".

- Place sleeve sts on holders as follows: Work to first raglan marker, drop marker, work 4 sts to center of cable and sl rem 4 sts of cable to st holder, drop next marker, sl sleeve sts to holder, drop next marker, sl first 4 sts of next cable to holder. Turn work and cable CO 8 (8, 10, 10, 12) sts for underarm. Turn work and cont to next marker, drop marker, work 4 sts to center of cable and sl rem 4 sts to new st holder, drop next marker, sl sleeve sts to holder, drop next marker, sl first 4 sts of next cable to holder. Turn work and cable CO 8 (8, 10, 10, 12) sts for underarm. Turn work and cont to last marker, drop marker, and finish row.

- Cont on body sts in St st to 11 (11½, 12, 12½, 13)" from beg of joined body.

- Change to size 8 needles and work in K2, P2 rib patt for 9 rnds, dec sts as needed to have rib patt come out evenly in first rnd. Change to B and work 1 rnd in K2, P2 rib patt. BO on next row with B in patt.

Sleeves

- Sl sts as if to purl from st holder to size 9 needles. Join A and cable CO 4 (4, 5, 5, 5, 6) sts at beg of next 2 rows for underarm.

- Work back and forth in St st using circular needle as a straight needle and dec 1 st at each end every 6 (6, 7, 7, 7) rows 4 times.

- Cont until sleeve is 5 (5, 6, 6, 6)" from PU row.

- Change to size 8 needles and work in K2, P2 rib patt for 6 rows.

- Change to B and work K2, P2 rib patt for 1 row. BO on next row with B in patt.

- Rep for 2nd sleeve.

Finishing

- Sew rem sleeve seam closed.
- Sew rem underarm seam closed.
- With size 9 needles and A, PU 84 (84, 96, 96, 96) sts around neck edge. Work in cabled rib patt for 1".
- Change to size 8 needles and cont in cable rib patt for 1".
- Change to B and work 1 row in K2, P2 rib patt. BO in patt on next row.

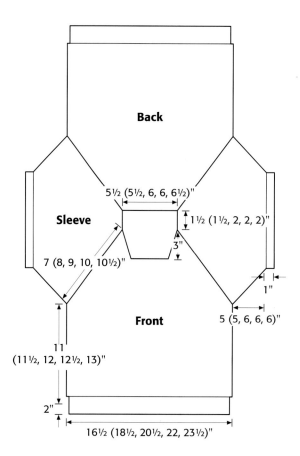

Changing the Look

Swatch A yarns: Trendsetter Aquarius (50 g, 110 yds), color 812, and Trendsetter Coconut (50 g, 65 yds), color 14

Aquarius is a slick ribbon that feels great against the body. The space-dyed colors are very subtle, allowing for easy color changes that move gracefully around the body. Coconut is used as the trim to add some frill and fun to a classic top-down sweater.

To make the sweater from these yarns, you'll need 5 (6, 7, 8, 9) skeins of Aquarius and 1 (1, 1, 1, 1) skein of Coconut.

Swatch B yarns: Muench Sir Galli (50 g, 104 yds), color 4911, and Muench Fabu (50 g, 79 yds), color 4303

I selected these two yarns because I wanted to show just how flexible this design can be. Sir Galli is a wonderful silk tweed that would be a great yarn for a year-round sweater and beautifully highlights the cable along the raglan. Fabu is fabulous and the texture along the edges will help to tickle your fancy.

To make the sweater with these yarns, you'll need 6 (7, 8, 9, 10) skeins of Sir Galli and 1 (1, 1, 1, 1) skein of Fabu.

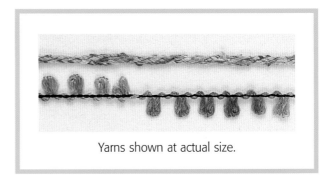

Yarns shown at actual size.

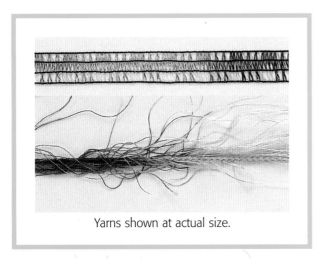

Yarns shown at actual size.

Swatch B

Swatch A

Café Chic: All Tied Up

Designed by Barry Klein

Knitting from the neck down in narrow stripes creates an interesting and fun tee. The narrow stripes enhance the shoulders because the corners turn over the body instead of around the body. I selected Dolcino as the base because the yarn has a great year-round feel and lots of elasticity so a good fit and easy style are ensured. Adding the multicolored texture and lash of Sorbet in the stripes adds that touch of "café chic" without going over the top.

Size:
Petite (Small, Medium, Large, X-Large)

Knitted Bust Measurement:
34 (37, 40, 43, 46)"

Materials

- **A** 8 (9, 10, 11, 12) skeins of Trendsetter Dolcino (50 g, 100 yds), color 8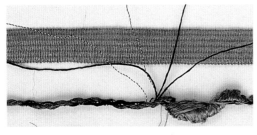
- **B** 2 (2, 2, 2, 2) skeins of Trendsetter Sorbet (50 g, 55 yds), color P-1051
- Size 10½ needles or size required to obtain gauge
- Size 10 needles
- Ring markers
- Stitch holders
- Size F crochet hook

Gauge:
16 sts and 21 rows = 4" in stripe patt on size 10½ needles

Yarns shown at actual size.

Stitch Patterns

Rib Pattern

Row 1: *K1, P1; rep from * across.

Row 2: Knit the knit sts and purl the purl sts.

Rep row 2.

Stripe Pattern

Rows 1 and 3 (RS): With A, knit.

Rows 2 and 4: With A, purl.

Row 5 (RS): With B, knit.

Row 6: With B, knit.

Rep rows 1–6 for stripe patt.

Body

- With size 10½ needles and A, CO 52 (58, 58, 64, 64) sts as follows: 1 st neck, 1 st front, pm, 2 sts raglan, pm, 8 (10, 10, 12, 12) sts shoulder/sleeve, pm, 2 sts raglan, pm, 24 (26, 26, 28, 28) sts back neck, pm, 2 sts raglan, pm, 8 (10, 10, 12, 12) sts shoulder/sleeve, pm, 2 sts raglan, pm, 1 st front, 1 st neck. Work in stripe patt, beg with row 2, inc 1 st (blind inc) on every RS row before and after each pair of markers, AT SAME TIME inc 1 st (blind inc) at neck edge every third row after first st on needle and just before last st on needle until sts for front and back sections are same.

Note: There will always be only 2 stitches between each pair of markers.

- Join work and cont in patt, working raglan inc only until raglan is 7 (7½, 8, 8½, 9)".
- Place sleeve sts on holders as follows: Work to first marker, drop marker, work 1 st, sl next st to holder, drop next marker, sl sleeve sts to holder, drop next marker, sl 1 st from raglan to holder. Turn work and cable CO 8 (10, 12, 12, 14) sts. Turn, work 1 st, drop next marker, work back body sts to next marker, drop marker, work 1 st, sl next st to new holder, drop marker, sl sleeve sts to

holder, drop next marker, sl 1 st to holder. Turn and cable CO 8 (10, 12, 12, 14) sts. Turn and work 1 st, drop next marker, work to beg.

- Cont on all body sts in knit only since work is now joined into 1 piece with sleeves on separate stitch holders. Work in A only until work is 11 (12, 12, 13, 13)" from joining.
- Change to size 10 needles, work in K1, P1 rib patt for 2". Change to B and BO in patt.

Sleeves

- With size 10½ needles, PU sleeve sts from first holder. Cont in stripe patt, join appropriate yarn, and cable CO 4 (5, 6, 6, 7) sts at beg of next 2 rows.
- Cont on all sts in stripe patt until sleeve is 4 (5, 5, 6, 6)" from PU and CO row.
- Change to size 10 needles and work in K1, P1 rib patt for 1". Change to B and BO in patt.
- Rep for 2nd sleeve.

Finishing

- Sew sleeve seam and side seams.
- With B, work 2 rows of sc around entire neck edge. Work 1 row of sl st around neck edge.

- Necktie (optional): With crochet hook and A, make a chain approx 50" long. Fasten off. Thread tails through each side of crochet at bottom of V, from inside to outside, like threading a pair of shoelaces. Work back and forth, crossing chains from one side to the other, moving up front toward neck and stopping 2" from top. Roll tails inward, winding them into a spiral and tack in place with a B tie so that tails will not pull back through.

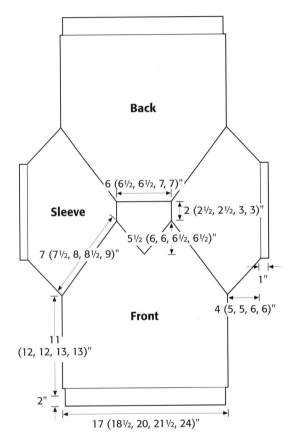

Changing the Look

Swatch A yarns: Muench Dynasty (50 g, 55 yds), color 20, and Muench String of Pearls (50 g, 99 yds), color 4016

I selected Dynasty for the base because it has many colors and textures. The luster of the metallic in String of Pearls became my accent or stripe yarn. Because String of Pearls is so thin, the accent stripes will be narrow, which will be more flattering to certain body types. For a bolder accent, you can always work 4 rows of garter stitch instead of 2.

To make the sweater from these yarns, you'll need 15 (16, 17, 18, 19) skeins of Dynasty and 1 (1, 1, 1, 2) skein of String of Pearls.

Swatch B yarns: Trendsetter Vintage (50 g, 80 yds), color 4367, and Trendsetter Dolcino (50 g, 100 yds), color 108

Vintage is a luxurious yarn, with soft, subtle color changes. It knits up like polar fleece. The accent stripes are toned down a bit and worked in garter stitch with Dolcino. Both yarns are the same gauge so you can work this sweater with either yarn as the base and create the ultimate wardrobe using the same yarns.

To make the sweater from these yarns, you'll need 10 (11, 12, 13, 14) skeins of Vintage and 1 (1, 1, 1, 2) skein of Dolcino.

Yarns shown at actual size.

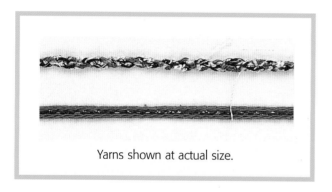

Yarns shown at actual size.

Swatch A

Swatch B

Glamour Girl: Luminary

Designed by Laura Bryant

Luminous indeed are the textures and colors used in this sweater made from "everything"—a great way to use up odds and ends and to try lots of different yarns. Using everything together gives a rich look without any one texture overpowering the others. Do you like glitz, but not too much? Want a little eyelash, but don't want to feel like a bear? This is the perfect place to try a little bit of this and a little bit of that. Dress it up—or dress it down. The choice is yours!

Size:

Small (Medium, Large, X-Large, XX-Large)

Knitted Bust Measurement:

35 (38, 42, 46, 50)"

Materials

900 (1000, 1150, 1300, 1500) yds of assorted yarns that work to a gauge of 5 sts per inch

We used:

- **A** 1 skein of Prism Trillino (2 oz, 85 yds), color Harvest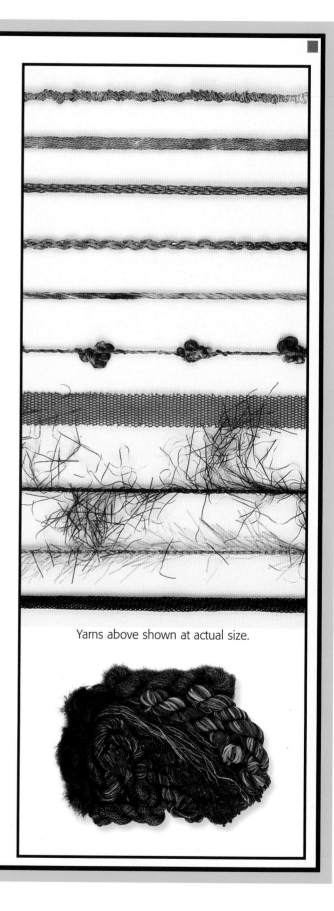
- **B** 1 skein of Prism Bon Bon (2 oz, 88 yds), color Tahoe
- **C** 1 skein of Prism Matte (1½ oz, 115 yds), color Orchard
- **D** 2 skeins of Prism Sunshine (1 oz, 65 yds), colors Tahoe, Nevada
- **E** 2 skeins of Prism Slique (1½ oz, 93 yds), colors Yosemite, Firefox
- **F** 2 skeins of Prism Biwa (1 oz, 68 yds), colors Autumn, Firefox
- **G** 1 skein of Prism Tulle (1 oz, 96 yds), color Tahoe
- **H** 1 skein of Prism Super Dazzle (1 oz, 90 yds), color Yosemite
- **I** 1 skein of Prism Dazzle (1 oz, 116 yds), color Orchard
- **Trim:** 1 skein of Prism Quicksilver (2 oz, 160 yds), color Autumn
- Size 6 circular needles or size required to obtain gauge
- Size F crochet hook
- Ring markers
- Stitch holders

Gauge:

21 sts and 30 rows = 4" in half linen st

Yarns above shown at actual size.

Half Linen Stitch

(even number of sts)

Row 1: *K1, sl 1 wyif; rep from * across.

Rows 2 and 4: Purl (this will become a knit row after you have joined for circular knitting).

Row 3: *Sl 1 wyif, K1; rep from * across.

About the pattern: As you increase, repeat row 1 on either side of yarn-over increase on every other right-side row (eliminating row 3). Once you have stopped increasing and are working the body in the round, the full 4 rows will be used, with rows 2 and 4 becoming knit rows.

About the color repeat: The entire garment is worked with 3 yarns at a time, one row of each yarn. Lay the yarns out in a pleasing order, selecting a smooth yarn such as Bon Bon as the first one, and alternate textures. Label yarns A, B, C, D, E, and so on, in order. Cast on with A, drop A and attach B, work across, drop B and attach C, and work back. When working a flat piece, A is waiting for you at the correct side. Once you have joined to work in the round, simply pass new yarn around the other 2 to bury them on the wrong side. After completing several inches, begin changing yarns: Cut A and attach D, then work B, C, D for 8 to 16 rows, then cut B and add E, working C, D, E for another 8 to 16 rows. Continue alternating textures and colors as desired. After placing sleeve stitches on a holder, reserve some yarn from the next few inches of the body for sleeves. After this, when working body, you may use up all of any one yarn, as it won't be needed again. To keep from building up bulk at beginning or end of rounds, cut and change yarns at various points in the body, burying the ends on the wrong side.

Body

- With A, CO 56 (58, 64, 66, 68) sts. Purl back and place markers: P2 front, pm, P1 raglan, pm, P10 (10, 12, 12, 12) shoulder/sleeve, pm, P1 raglan, pm, P28 (30, 32, 34, 36) back neck, pm, P1 raglan, pm, P10 (10, 12, 12, 12) shoulder/sleeve, pm, P1 raglan, pm, P2 front.

- Add B, beg half linen st, and establish inc: Work 2 sts, YO, slip marker, K1, slip marker, YO, work 10 (10, 12, 12, 12) sts, YO, slip marker, K1, slip marker, YO, work 28 (30, 32, 34, 36) sts, YO, slip marker, K1, slip marker, YO, work 10 (10, 12, 12, 12) sts, YO, slip marker, K1, slip marker, YO, work 2 sts.

- **Next row:** Add C and purl 1 row.

- **Next row:** With A, K1f&b in first st, work row 1 of patt to first marker, YO, slip marker, K1, slip marker, YO, work row 1 of patt, and inc as established with YO before and after each pair of markers, always keeping st between as knit st, end with K1f&b in last st.

- **Next row:** With B, purl back.

- Using 3-yarn rotation, cont to work a YO on each side of each pair of markers as established and AT SAME TIME inc at front edge 1 st EOR 11 (12, 13, 14, 15) times—54 (58, 62, 66, 70) sts each on front or back. each on front or back.

- Join to work in rnd, cont in current color for at least 1 more row. Beg changing colors at random points within body (instead of lining them up), and bury ends as you work.

- Cont in rnd to approx 7 (7½, 8, 8½, 9)". There should be 80 (88, 96, 104, 112) sts each for front and back.

- Join for body and place sleeve sts on holders as follows: Work across front sts, cable CO 12 (12, 14, 18, 20) sts, drop marker, sl next st to holder, drop marker, sl sleeve sts to holder, drop marker, sl next st to holder, drop marker, work across back, cable CO 12 (12, 14, 18, 20) sts; drop marker, sl next st to new holder, drop marker, sl sleeve sts to holder, drop marker, sl next st to holder, drop marker—184 (200, 220, 244, 264) sts.

- Cont on body sts to a total length of 20 (21, 22, 23, 24)", holding work upright while measuring to allow for downward stretch. BO all sts loosely.

Sleeves

- CO 6 (6, 7, 9, 10) sts, work sleeve sts from holder, cable CO 6 (6, 7, 9, 10) sts at beg of next row.
- Working back and forth, cont in patt in color sequence as for body, dec 1 st at each edge every 4th row 7 (7, 8, 8, 9) times; sleeve should be approx 3½ (3½, 4, 4, 4½)" long from CO and PU row. BO all sts loosely.
- Rep for second sleeve.

Finishing

- Sew any seams (sleeve, underarm, or side).
- With trim yarn, work 1 rnd sc and 1 rnd rev sc around bottom edge of body and sleeves. Work 2 rnds sc and then 1 rnd rev sc around neck edge.

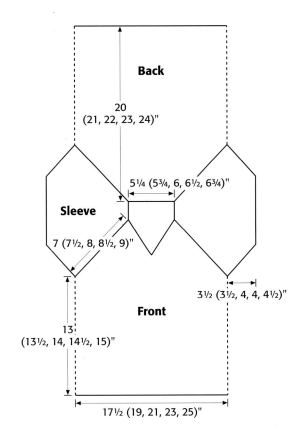

Changing the Look

Swatch A yarns: Muench Bali (50 g, 160 yds), color 31 (A); Muench Serpentine (50 g, 143 yds), color 906 (B); Prism Biwa (1 oz, 65 yds), color Fog (C)

Three yarns used as A, B, C for the entire garment give a more tailored, less flashy look. The multicolors of Fog are blended with lavender Bali and soft teal Serpentine, while the bumpy texture of Biwa is highlighted by smooth, matte Bali and smooth, shiny Serpentine, which also becomes the perfect edge.

To make the sweater from these three yarns, you'll need 2 (2, 3, 3, 4) skeins of Bali; 2 (3, 3, 4, 4) skeins of Serpentine (extra allowed for the edging); and 5 (5, 6, 7, 8) skeins of Biwa.

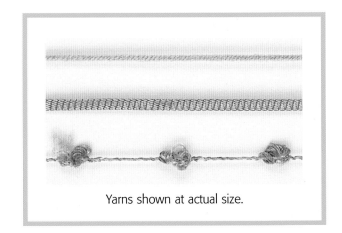

Yarns shown at actual size.

Swatch B yarns:

- Trendsetter Taos (50 g, 110 yds), color 293 (A)
- Trendsetter Sunshine (50 g, 95 yds), color 39
- Trendsetter Aura (50 g, 148 yds), color 8293
- Trendsetter Flora (20 g, 77 yds), color 9000
- Trendsetter Charm (20 g, 94 yds), color 03
- Trendsetter Binario (25 g, 82 yds), color 113

A more muted palette lends sophisticated elegance to this swatch. Taos, with its hint of pastel color, is used as A and never changes, while the other 5 yarns take turns with one another. Taos is then used to trim the edge for continuity.

To make the sweater from these yarns, you'll need 3 (4, 5, 5, 6) skeins of Taos (allows extra for edging) and enough yardage of the other yarns (in any combination) to reach a total of 600 (660, 770, 870, 1000) yds.

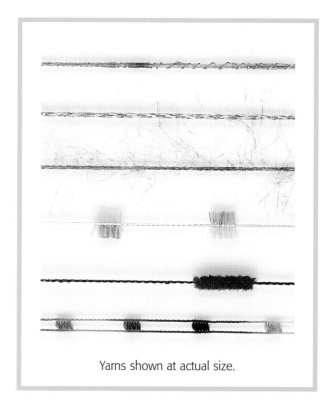

Yarns shown at actual size.

Swatch A

Swatch B

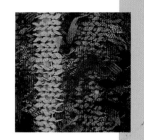

A Sideways View

Who doesn't love vertical stripes? The up-and-down direction when stripes are knitted side to side makes this a great selection for someone seeking a slimming look. Whether wide, thin, gradated, or random, vertical stripes carry the eye up, not across.

Beginning at the sleeve edge, you can knit straight up the sleeve and across the body of a tee, dividing the front and back for the neck opening. The only seam to be sewn will be the side/underarm and sleeve seam. Long-sleeved sweaters can be difficult when constructed this way because the weight of the sleeves tends to pull too much on the shoulder area, which is not reinforced with a seam. For a short-sleeved tee, however, the concept is great. If the yarn you choose is very heavy, consider putting a seam in the shoulder (knit the sleeve/front and sleeve/back in 1 piece each, then seam the shoulders and continue right down the middle of the sleeve). This will help support the knitting and keep it more stable. Another option is to knit the sweater in 4 pieces: front, back, and 2 sleeves, with each piece being knit from the side edge instead of from the bottom or top. This is better for heavier yarns because the seams add stability.

Side-to-side knitting will behave somewhat differently when worn. Stitches turned sideways tend to stretch a bit more, so we have taken that into account when writing our patterns. Plan on the garments growing in length from their original knitted dimension. We also suggest knitting most yarns a bit tighter than one normally would, to help control the stretch factor.

Design Options

Side-to-side knitting automatically suggests stripes, and since they will be vertical, they are flattering to most everyone. Simple pattern stitches are well suited, but elaborate ones are probably better worked from the bottom up as the stretch factor may distort

the appearance of the stitch. Stitch patterns with strong verticals (such as lines of cables) will become horizontal when knit side to side, so these may not be the best option. Side-to-side knitting is perfect for fringed garments, such as in Bandstand on page 75, because you can cut and tie yarn ends as you knit, with only a trim needed to even them out later.

Yarn Suggestions

Lighter-weight yarns will reduce stretching, as will more resilient yarn (it will show some elasticity when a strand is pulled taut). This type of knitting is great for textured yarns when they are used as accents.

Fit Tips

Length adjustments must be made by changing the number of cast-on body stitches. Remember that garments knit from side to side will tend to grow in length.

X **Generally flattering:** It is, however, difficult to show waist definition.

V **Generally flattering:** It may be loose around hips when knit to accommodate bust. A band can be added to bring the bottom edge in. If working in stripes, the finished bust measurement should be large enough so stripes don't wave as they move over the bust.

∧ **The best way for you to use stripes:** Shorter lengths will be better, and consider leaving side vents open to accommodate fuller hips. Sleeves with a modified drop shoulder are better than all-in-one-piece sleeves and body, as they bring the shoulder line to a more natural position.

II **This is the perfect style for you!**

Techniques: Beyond Getting Started

Refer to the following instructions as needed to complete your garment.

Self-Fringing

To work fringe as you knit, as in Bandstand on page 75, cut the yarn from the row just worked, leaving an end about 6" long. Lay the new yarn alongside the old, even up the ends, and tie an overhand knot: make a loop and draw the ends through the loop, tightening the knot against the knitting. Work another row and repeat the fringe. Trim evenly after all knitting is finished, seamed, and beaded if desired.

Beading

Beads need to have large-enough holes for the yarn strands to fit through, but just barely, so that you can tie a knot to keep the bead on. Again, use an overhand knot, but instead of pulling the end through just once, wrap the end through several times to make a thicker knot. Place all beads on fringe before trimming ends, as the strands will get shorter when you tie the knots.

Casual Comfort: Playful

Designed by Barry Klein and Fayla Reiss

The name for this sweater truly expresses my feelings about the design and the yarns that we used; everything is playful. When trying to design something for a side-to-side sweater, we had to look at yarns that would not stretch or grow, yet would feel soft and move with the body. Iguana is just that—a supple, plied yarn in wonderful, bright colors, each wrapped with a black binder. Siam has a woven ribbon base with soft, short lashes that pull out the texture and bring additional life to the design. The side vents allow for a truly casual feel and a fit that is good for every body style. Throw on some black jeans and wear this sweater—get playful!

Size:

Small (Medium, Large, X-Large)

Knitted Bust Measurement:
36 (39, 42, 45)"

Materials

- **MC** 5 (6, 7, 8) skeins of Trend-setter Siam (50 g, 110 yds), color 5014 [4]
- **A** 2 (2, 2, 2) skeins of Trendsetter Iguana (50 g, 82 yds), color 840 Turquoise [4]
- **B** 2 (2, 2, 2) skeins of Trendsetter Iguana, color 839 Purple
- **C** 2 (2, 2, 2) skeins of Trendsetter Iguana, color 842 Copper
- Size 8 needles or size required to obtain gauge
- Size G crochet hook

Gauge:
16 sts and 24 rows = 4" in rev St st

Yarns shown at actual size.

Body

Knit from sleeve to sleeve in 1 piece.

- With MC, CO 48 (50, 52, 54) sts. Work small stripe patt in rev St st, inc 1 st at each end every 7 (6, 6, 5) rows 4 (5, 6, 7) times— 56 (60, 64, 68) sts.

Small stripe patt: Work 2 rows with MC, 2 rows with A, 2 rows with MC, 2 rows with B, 2 rows with MC, 2 rows with C.

- Change to MC and cont in rev St st until sleeve is 6½ (6½, 7, 7)" from CO.
- Change to large stripe patt, AT SAME TIME cable CO 48 (50, 52, 54) sts at beg of next 2 rows—152 (160, 168, 176) sts.

Large stripe patt: Work 4 rows with C, 2 rows with MC, 4 rows with B, 2 rows with MC, 4 rows with A, 2 rows with MC.

- Rep large stripe patt to approx 5½ (6¼, 7, 7¾)" from body CO, ending with stripe C, B, or A.
- Change to medium stripe patt and AT SAME TIME, work across 70 (74, 78, 82) sts, join 2nd ball of yarn and BO center 12 sts to create a neck opening for front and back. Finish row.

Medium stripe patt: Work 4 rows with MC, 2 rows with C, 4 rows with MC, 2 rows with B, 4 rows with MC, 2 rows with A.

- Rep medium stripe patt until center neck area is approx 7" from BO, end ready for MC stripe.
- Change to new large stripe patt and AT SAME TIME work up to neck split and drop yarn. Using yarn from next piece, cable CO 12 sts. Cut yarn and, using attached yarn, work across entire row, joining work into 1 piece again.

New large stripe patt: Work 2 rows with MC, 4 rows with C, 2 rows with MC, 4 rows with B, 2 rows with MC, 4 rows with A.

- Rep new large stripe patt until side panel is approx 5½ (6¼, 7, 7¾)" from front/back joining, end ready for row 3 of color C, B, or A.
- BO 48 (50, 52, 54) sts at beg of next 2 rows.

- **Beg sleeve:** Change to MC, cont in rev St st for 8 (6, 6, 8) rows, dec 1 st at each end on next row and then every 7 (6, 6, 5) rows 3 (4, 5, 6) more times.
- When sleeve is 4½ (4½, 5, 5)", change to new small stripe patt and cont sleeve shaping.

New small stripe patt: Work 2 rows with C, 2 rows with MC, 2 rows with B, 2 rows with MC, 2 rows with A, 2 rows with MC.

- BO on next row.

Finishing

- Fold front over back, centering the neck edge, and sew underarm and side seams closed, leaving an open side vent of 3" to 4" at bottom edge of each side as desired.
- With Siam, work 1 row of sc and 1 row of sl-st crochet along bottom edges and side-vent openings. Rep same 2 rows of crochet around neck edge.

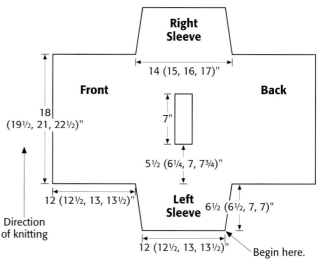

Changing the Look ▪ ▪ ▪

Swatch A yarns: Trendsetter Siam (50 g, 110 yds), color 903 (MC), and Trendsetter Spiral (50 g, 110 yds), colors 107 (A), 96 (B), 103 (C)

Siam is the same as I used in the original. This time, I thought about reversing the striping by working the lash yarn in a multi-color and making solid stripes in Spiral. When this was done, I looked at the swatch and decided that I liked the stripe definition in this combination, so I put the stockinette or knit side out as my right side.

To make the sweater in these yarns, you'll need 5 (6, 7, 8) skeins of Siam and 2 (2, 2, 2) skeins each of A, B, and C in Spiral.

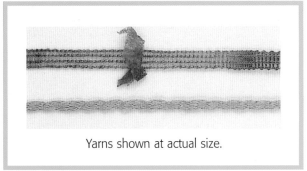

Yarns shown at actual size.

Swatch B yarns: Trendsetter Aquarius (50 g, 95 yds), color 818 (MC), and Trendsetter Safari (50 g, 72 yds), color 4055 (substitute for A, B, and C)

As much as I loved the original, I love how these two yarns match so closely in color, allowing the textures to play off of each other. You get just enough of Safari's texture to enjoy both yarns and not lose the stripes.

To make the sweater in these yarns, you'll need 6 (7, 8, 9) skeins of Aquarius and 7 (7, 7, 7) skeins of Safari.

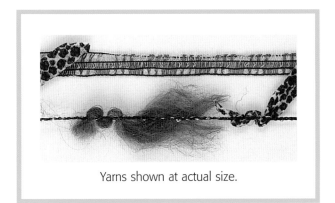

Yarns shown at actual size.

Swatch A

Swatch B

Workaday Wear:
Made in the Shade

Designed by Laura Bryant

Shades of sophistication—three landscape colors blend one to another across this tailored tee. Since it is knit all in one piece, minimal finishing lets you wear your creation soon! The subtle shading is achieved using Fibonacci numbers (a sequence of numbers found in nature) for a smooth transition. Any adjustments needed for sizing can be made by working more or fewer rows in the plain areas. Bon Bon, a smooth rayon tape, creates a fabric that is sleek, yet crisp.

Size:

Small (Medium, Large, X-Large, XX-Large)

Knitted Bust Measurement:

34 (38, 42, 46, 50)"

Materials

- **Prism Bon Bon** (2 oz, 88 yds) in the following amounts and colors: **3**
  - **A** 3 (3, 4, 4, 5) skeins, color 312 Soft Teal
  - **B** 3 (4, 4, 5, 6) skeins, color 310 Sage Green
  - **C** 3 (3, 4, 4, 5) skeins, color 307 Khaki
- Size 6 needles or size required to obtain gauge
- Size 4 needles
- Size 4 circular needles
- Size F crochet hook

Gauge:

20 sts and 26 rows = 4" in St st on size 6 needles

Yarn shown at actual size.

Stripe pattern: Tee is worked in 1 piece from side to side, following the stripe pattern to form gradations. The stripe pattern is dependent on row gauge, but if yours is different, you can adjust the stripes slightly to correct, or just work more or less of color B in the center. Measurements are given in the pattern directions to help you with this. The stripe pattern is the same for each size; the difference in sizing is made up for in the large areas between stripes and in the sleeves.

Stripe Pattern in Stockinette Stitch

1 row with B
13 rows with A
1 row with B
8 rows with A
2 rows with B
5 rows with A
3 rows with B
3 rows with A
5 rows with B
2 rows with A
8 rows with B
1 row with A
13 rows with B

Work even as directed in patt, then rep stripe patt, substituting C for B and B for A.

Body

Knit from left sleeve to right sleeve in 1 piece.

- With size 4 needles and A, CO 54 (58, 62, 66, 68) sts. Work 6 rows in garter st.
- Change to St st and size 6 needles, inc 1 st at each edge every 4th row 7 times—68 (72, 76, 80, 82) sts. AT SAME TIME, after 5 (6, 7, 8, 9)", beg stripe patt. When sleeve is 6 (7, 8, 9, 10)", cable CO 66 (68, 72, 75, 76) sts for body at beg of next 2 rows—200 (208, 220, 230, 234) sts.
- Cont in stripe patt, work to 5½ (6½, 7¼, 8, 9)" from body CO row, then divide and shape neck: Work across 100 (104, 110,

115, 117) sts, join 2nd ball of yarn and BO 3 sts, finish row.

- Work back as established and work front as follows: BO 2 sts at beg of next 2 RS rows, dec 1 st at beg of every RS row 5 times.
- Work even to 8½ (9½, 10½, 11½, 12½)" from body CO row, mark for center front.

Note: Check where you are in the stripe sequence: For small, you should be about in the middle of 13 rows of B. For larger sizes, work as many extra rows of B as necessary to get to the correct measurement.

- Work same number of B rows as you worked after last A row. Beg shading to color C by working first C row, following stripe patt, AT SAME TIME reverse neck shaping by increasing and then casting on sts with cable CO. Rejoin front and back when shaping is complete.

- When body is 17 (19, 21, 23, 25)" across, BO 66 (68, 72, 75, 76) sts at beg of next 2 rows.
- Work 2nd sleeve, reversing shaping and finishing sleeve with color C.

Finishing

- Sew side and sleeve seams.
- With B, work 1 rnd sc and 1 rnd rev sc around neck edge.
- With size 4 circular needles and B, PU 200 (220, 240, 260, 280) sts around bottom edge. Work 6 rows of garter st in rnds (purl 1 rnd, knit 1 rnd), then BO firmly but not tightly (edge should lie flat, not pull in or waver).

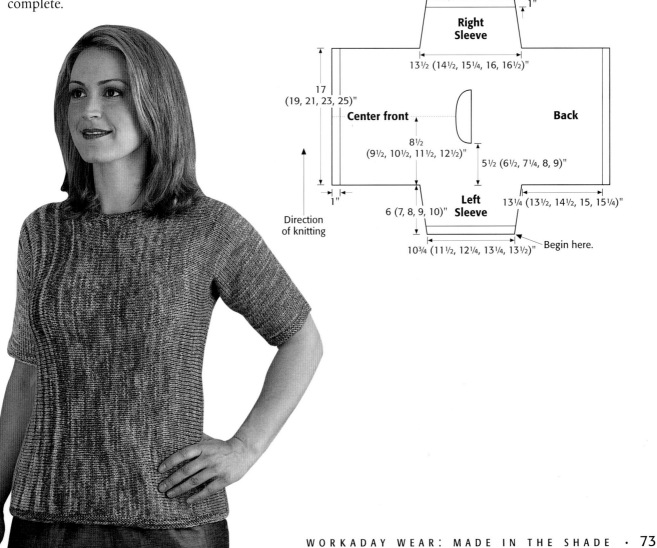

Changing the Look

Swatch A yarn: Muench Velour (25 g, 64 yds), colors 5 (A), 7 (B), 8 (C)

The softly sueded surface of Velour imparts a more rustic style to this swatch—perfect with a suede skirt or pants! The tone-on-tone dyeing adds to the napped surface and mimics the look of our Bon Bon model.

To make this sweater with Velour, you'll need 4 (5, 6, 6, 7) skeins of A; 4 (5, 6, 7, 9) skeins of B; and 4 (5, 6, 6, 7) skeins of C.

Yarn shown at actual size.

Swatch A

Swatch B yarn: Trendsetter Spiral (50 g, 110 yds), colors 91 (A), 191 (B), 201 (C)

An interesting wrapped texture enhances and plays up the subtle tweediness of Spiral. The matte core of the yarn is wrapped in a shiny filament of slightly different colors. Strongly contrasting neutrals make this swatch more dynamic than the closely related colors in the model.

To make this sweater with Spiral, you'll need 3 (3, 4, 4, 4) skeins of A; 3 (4, 4, 5, 5) skeins of B; and 3 (3, 4, 4, 4) skeins of C.

Yarn shown at actual size.

Swatch B

Café Chic: Bandstand

Designed by Laura Bryant

Strike up the band, indeed! Make a grand entrance with this playful striped and fringed tee. Shades of denim blue are fringed for an urban cowgirl look and beaded for the '60s girl in you. The fringe is made as the tee is knit, and fringe at the bottom edge and at the neck and shoulder make a strong statement. Too much fringe for you? Bury the ends at the shoulder and neck for a more refined look.

Size:

Small (Medium, Large, X-Large)

Knitted Bust Measurement:

Approx 36 (40, 44, 48)"

Materials

- **A** 4 (4, 5, 6) skeins of Prism Bon Bon (2 oz, 88 yds), color 111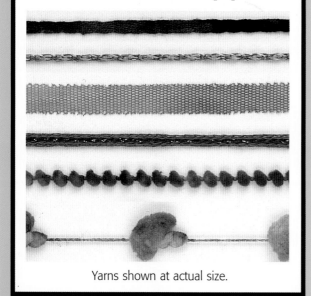
- **B** 1 (2, 2, 3) skeins of Trendsetter Sunshine (50 g, 93 yds), color 060
- **C** 1 (2, 2, 3) skeins of Prism Tulle (1 oz, 96 yds), color Denim
- **D** 1 (2, 2, 3) skeins of Muench String of Pearls (50 g, 99 yds), color 4022
- **E** 1 (2, 2, 2) skeins of Prism Pebbles (2 oz, 123 yds), color Denim
- **F** 2 (3, 3, 3) skeins of Prism Bubbles (2 oz, 68 yds), color Denim
- Size 8 needles or size required to obtain gauge
- Size F crochet hook

Optional:

- 3 dozen Prism Fimo beads; 6 dozen large-hole glass beads

Gauge:

16 sts and 30 rows = 4" in stripe patt

Yarns shown at actual size.

Stripe Pattern

Cast on with A.

Row 1: With A, knit.

Row 2: With C, purl.

Row 3: With B, knit.

Row 4: With D, purl.

Rows 5 and 6: With E, knit.

Row 7: With B, knit.

Row 8: With C, purl.

Row 9: With D, knit.

Row 10: With A, purl.

Rows 11 and 12: With F, knit.

Rep these 12 rows for stripe patt.

To make fringe, at each yarn change, cut yarn, leaving a tail approx 6" long. Tie new yarn to end with a tail of equal length. This will become the fringe at both top and bottom.

Back

- Beg at left back side seam with A, CO 38 (40, 42, 44) sts. Work in stripe patt, making fringe at bottom edge (beg of RS rows). Work for 2 (2½, 3, 4)", then at beg next WS row cable CO 32 (34, 36, 38) sts—70 (74, 78, 82) sts.
- Cont in stripe patt to 16 (17½, 19, 20)", then at beg next WS row BO 32 (34, 36, 38) sts.
- Cont on 38 (40, 43, 44) sts for 2 (2½, 3, 4)". BO all sts.

Front

- Work as for back to 6¼ (7, 7¾, 8½)" from beg.
- **Shape neck:** BO 6 (7, 8, 8) sts at neck edge, then at beg of next WS rows, BO 2 sts once, 2 sts again, then dec 1 st at neck edge EOR 4 times.
- Work to 9 (10, 11, 12)" from beg, mark for center front, reverse neck shaping by inc, then casting on sts with cable CO.
- Cont in stripe patt as for back to 16 (17½, 19, 20)", then BO 32 (34, 36, 38) sts.
- Cont on 38 (40, 43, 44) sts for 2 (2½, 3, 4)". BO all sts.

Sleeves

- With A, CO 16 (16, 18, 18) sts. Work stripe patt as for body, without leaving fringe (you will begin making fringe again when all short-row shaping is complete). Work short row shaping as follows: Work 4 sts, turn, sl 1, work 3 sts, turn, work 8 sts, turn, sl 1, turn, work to end, turn, work 12 sts, turn, sl 1, turn, work to end, turn, work to end (sleeve taper made). Resume making fringe at bottom edge only and work to 17 (17½, 18, 18½)", measured along the long edge.
- Reverse short-row shaping by working BO 4 sts at beg of next 3 RS rows, then BO 4 (4, 6, 6) sts.

Finishing

- Place front and back WS together. With A, work 1 row sc across shoulder seam, pushing all fringe to RS of front or back as you work. Work 1 row rev sc along shoulder. Fringe should fall to front and back appropriately.
- Sew sleeve to CO edge of armhole opening. Tack edge of sleeve to underarm of body.
- Sew sleeve and side seams.
- With A, work 1 rnd sc and 1 rnd rev sc around neck edge, pushing all fringe to right side.
- Attach beads to fringe as desired. When all beads are attached, trim fringe to approx 3".

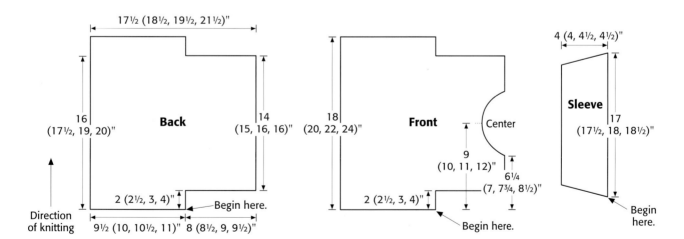

Changing the Look

Swatch A yarns:

- Filatura Di Crosa Venus (50 g, 83 yds), color 38 (A)
- Filatura di Crosa Sesamo (50 g, 71 yds), color 18 (B)
- Tahki Lily (50 g, 135 yds), color 002 (C)
- Filatura di Crosa Ananas (50 g, 55 yds), color 107 (D)
- Filatura di Crosa Giardino (50 g, 70 yds), color 104 (E)
- Muench Yarns Fabu (50 g, 78 yds), color M4305 (F)

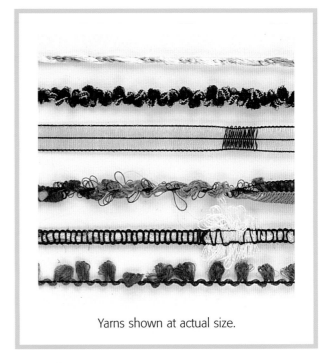

Yarns shown at actual size.

Here you find a different kind of neutral: black and white with bare hints of color. This tee would go as well with jeans as with dressy black slacks. The little flowers in Giardino bring a breath of fresh air to this look and are a great substitute for the popcorn of Bubbles. Fabu brings a different texture to the mix, and the other tapes and ribbons each have their own personality. Watch the fringe—if the yarns tend to fray or unravel, either tie a tight knot at the end of each strand, or dab a touch of Fray Check on the ends.

To make the sweater from these yarns, you'll need 4 (4, 5, 6) skeins of Venus A; 2 (3, 3, 4) skeins of Sesamo B; 1 (2, 2, 2) skein of Lily C; 2 (3, 4, 5) skeins of Ananas D; 2 (3, 4, 4) skeins of Giardino E; and 2 (2, 3, 3) skeins of Fabu F.

Swatch A

Swatch B yarns:

- Filatura Di Crosa Brilla (50 g, 120 yds), color 307 (A)
- Filatura di Crosa Venus (50 g, 83 yds), color 22 (B)
- Trendsetter Aura (50 g, 148 yds), color 63 (C)
- Stacy Charles Asti (50 g, 81 yds), color 3 (D)
- Stacy Charles Cancun (50 g, 93 yds), color 86 (E)
- Trendsetter Siam (50 g, 110 yds), color 2506 (F)

Heat up the color and the texture for a jazzy, dressier version of this tee. Bright summery colors, playful textures and a bit of sparkle make this a favorite for warm weather nights. Pale gold Aura adds glitter and shine, but almost disappears as a color. Solid burnt orange Brilla grounds the fanciful confetti colors of the remaining yarns, allowing the texture to speak while keeping the overall look from becoming neon bright.

To make the sweater from these yarns, you'll need 3 (3, 4, 5) skeins of Brilla A; 1 (2, 3, 4) skeins of Venus B; 1 (2, 2, 3) skeins of Aura C; 1 (2, 3, 4) skeins of Asti D; 2 (3, 3, 3) skeins of Cancun E; and 2 (2, 2, 2) skeins of Siam F.

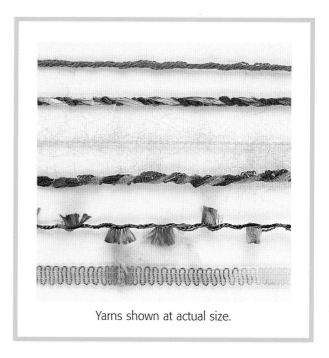

Yarns shown at actual size.

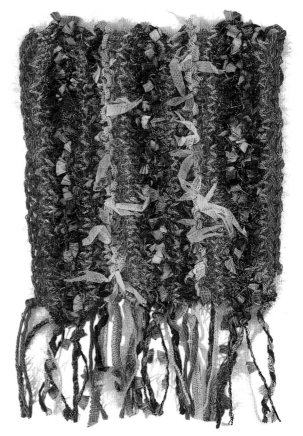

Swatch B

Glamour Girl: Sheer Delight

Designed by Barry Klein and Fayla Reiss

With the knitting talents of my good friend Fayla Reiss, we went about creating a side-to-side sweater that would work for all sizes and look great on the "glamour girl." The original sketches had stripes all the way across and the fabric was not as sheer. As Fayla began to work the sweater, it became apparent that the sheerness was important to the lightness of the sweater. It also became a lovely background for the beautiful flowers that decorate the tie at the shoulder. The lack of stripes on the body keeps the sweater slimming, and the stripes on the sleeve open up the yoke and bring the eyes up to the face. Don't you just love it!

Body

Knit from left sleeve to right sleeve in 1 piece.

- With size 6 needles and B, CO 54 (58, 62, 66, 70) sts. Work following stripe patt in rev St st, inc 1 st at each end every 4th row 6 times—66 (70, 74, 78, 82) sts.

  > 5 rows with B
  >
  > (2 rows with A, 2 rows with B, 2 rows with MC) 1 (1, 2, 2, 3) times
  >
  > 2 rows with A
  >
  > 2 rows with B
  >
  > 4 rows with MC
  >
  > 2 rows with A
  >
  > 2 rows with B
  >
  > 6 rows with MC
  >
  > 2 rows with A
  >
  > 2 rows with B

- Change to MC and cont in rev St st until sleeve is 6 (6, 7, 7, 8)". Note how many additional rows are worked after final stripe so that other sleeve will match.

- Change to size 7 needles and with MC only, cable CO 54 sts at beg of next 2 rows for body—174 (178, 182, 186, 190) sts.

- Cont in rev St st to 4½ (5½, 6½, 7½, 8½)" from body CO row, end ready for purl row.

- Work 79 (81, 83, 85, 87) sts for front, join second ball of yarn, BO next 16 sts for neck edge, finish row.

- Work front and back at same time with separate skeins of yarn for 8", end ready for a purl row.

- Purl across front sts. Drop yarn. Using yarn from back, cable CO 16 sts to fill in neck-edge opening. Break yarn from back and work across CO sts with yarn from front, joining both pieces into 1 again, with 174 (178, 182, 186, 190) sts on needle.

- Cont in rev St st for 4½ (5½, 6½, 7½, 8½)" from neck CO.

- BO 54 sts at beg of next 2 rows.

- Change to size 6 needles, cont with MC in rev St st, working same number of rows on

Size:

Petite (Small, Medium, Large, X-Large)

Knitted Bust Measurement:

34 (38, 42, 46, 50)"

Materials

- **MC** 6 (7, 8, 9, 10) skeins of Trendsetter Binario (25 g, 82 yds), color 123

- **A** 2 (2, 2, 2, 2) skeins of Trendsetter Sunshine (50 g, 95 yds), color 31 Forest Green

- **B** 1 (1, 1, 1, 1) skein of Trendsetter Sunshine, color 06 Citrus

- 1 yard of Trendsetter Flower Garden, color 123

- Size 7 needles or size required to obtain gauge

- Size 6 needles

- Size F crochet hook

Gauge:

18 sts and 24 rows = 4" in rev St st on size 7 needles

Yarns shown at actual size.

all sts as worked for other sleeve after final stripe.

- Beg following stripe patt, dec 1 st at each end every 4th row 6 times—54 (58, 62, 66, 70) sts.

      2 rows with B
      2 rows with A
      6 rows with MC
      2 rows with B
      2 rows with A
      4 rows with MC
      2 rows with B
      2 rows with A
      (2 rows with MC, 2 rows with B,
          2 rows with A) 1 (1, 2, 2, 3) times

- Change to B and cont in rev St st for 5 rows. BO all sts.

Finishing

- Fold sweater in half, placing front over back, and sew underarm seams closed.

- With B, work 1 rnd of sc around bottom edge. Work 1 row of sl-st crochet, working into back half of each st around bottom to bring edge in and add a soft ridge.

- With size 7 needles and B, CO 8 sts. Work in St st until piece is 48" long, BO. Fold strip in half and pin center of strip to right neck-edge corner. Sew 1 edge of strip around neck edge, working 1 strip along front neck and 1 strip along back neck, ending both strips at center edge of left front neck edge. Fold strip over lengthwise and sew remaining opening of strip closed to create a tube. Place 1 strip over the other and tie both together into an overhand knot. Sew knot in place on left front edge, allowing balance of strips to hang down. Lay flower strip along 1 knit strip. Carefully cut flower strip 1" shorter than knit strip. With sewing thread, attach flower strip to knit strip, working from the knot down. Rep for other knit strip.

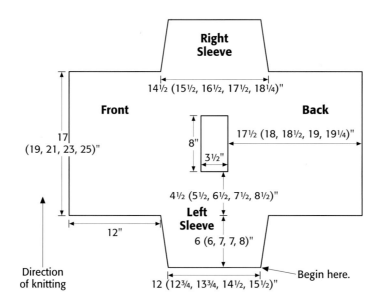

14½ (15½, 16½, 17½, 18¼)"

Right Sleeve

Front

Back

17 (19, 21, 23, 25)"

8"

3½"

17½ (18, 18½, 19, 19¼)"

4½ (5½, 6½, 7½, 8½)"

Left Sleeve

6 (6, 7, 7, 8)"

12"

Direction of knitting

12 (12¾, 13¾, 14½, 15½)"

Begin here.

Changing the Look ■ ■ ■

Swatch A yarn: Trendsetter Flora (20 g, 77 yds), color 202 (MC), and Trendsetter Sunshine (50 g, 95 yds), color 53 (substitute for A and B)

Flora is one of the most wonderful components for a garment and only recently have we been using it all on its own. The yarn has small flags that are close together, keeping the sheer look that the original design has, but now bringing up more texture. Sunshine is used exactly the same as in the original—a bright solid accent that details the stripes.

To make the sweater from Flora, you'll need 7 (8, 9, 10, 11) skeins of Flora and 2 (2, 2, 2, 2) skeins of Sunshine.

Yarn shown at actual size.

Swatch A

Swatch B yarns: Prism Wild Stuff (8 oz, 300 yds), color Nevada (MC), and Prism Bon Bon (2 oz, 88 yds), color Nevada (substitute for A and B)

Because Wild Stuff has so many wonderful textures in one hank, the sideways stripes will be narrow and the color changes and textures will flow across the body. Bon Bon is a woven ribbon that is the same gauge as, and is dyed to match, Wild Stuff. Because there is so much texture, the matching Bon Bon creates a textured stripe rather than a color stripe.

To make the sweater, you'll need 1½ (1½, 2, 2, 2½) hanks of Wild Stuff and 3 (3, 3, 3, 3) skeins of Bon Bon.

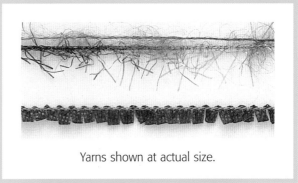

Yarns shown at actual size.

Swatch B

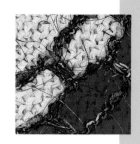

Dynamite Diagonals

Make knitting magic! When worked on the bias, stripes become active design elements. Since you are knitting to a measurement, the gauge isn't critical to garment fit, making this a great choice for anyone who has trouble maintaining or achieving gauge. You just need to have a good tape measure and a flat surface on which to spread out your knitting as you work.

Diagonal knitting is created by beginning in one corner of a piece with one stitch and increasing along both edges to create the side legs of the rectangle or square. Once the desired width is reached, you can continue to increase along one edge and begin to decrease along the other until the desired length is reached. At this point, both edges will be decreased down to one stitch remaining—piece completed!

The trick to successful diagonal knitting is in understanding the stitch-to-row ratio, since this will determine the rate of increasing and decreasing necessary to create a square corner. Most diagonal knitting failures can be traced back to the corners being oblique, not square, which causes the seams to twist around the body instead of lying flat along the sides.

Bias Knitting in Garter Stitch

This is the easiest kind of diagonal knitting to work, because the stitch-to-row ratio in garter stitch is almost always 1:2; that is, there are twice as many rows as there are stitches to equal an inch. The rate of increase and then decrease will be every other row—half of the rows being knit. The easiest way to keep track of this is to work the shaping at the beginning of every row. This achieves the same result as working both actions in one row, then working a row even. Remember that garter stitch has no visible right or wrong side, so trying to keep track of right- and wrong-side rows can become difficult. Placing a safety pin on the right side can help you keep track. If you are working one-row stripes on the bias, garter stitch will make them less distinct and more blended.

Bias Knitting in Stockinette Stitch

Stockinette stitch is a bit trickier to figure because the stitches and rows don't always have a nice, neat ratio. However, we have found that most ratios are very close to 2:3, which results in an increase rate of 2 out of 3 rows. So, the pattern would be a 6-row repeat:

Row 1: Knit, inc 1 st at each end.
Row 2: Purl, inc 1 st at each end.
Row 3: Knit (no shaping).
Row 4: Rep row 2.
Row 5: Rep row 1.
Row 6: Purl (no shaping).

The nice thing is that even if you lose your place and get the occasional row out of order, as long as most of your shaping is done to the above formula, your work will be square enough.

If you are like Laura and tuck your legs under your body while sitting and knitting, here is a handy hint for keeping track of your increase rows: when you end your knitting session, always finish with a row 3 or 6 (work-even row). When you pick it up again, you will know that the next 2 rows are increase rows. If the knit side is facing, tuck your right leg under. When you come back to the next knit row, it is a work-even row, and your right leg tells you that. If a purl row is facing, tuck your left leg. After the 2 increase rows, a purl row will be the next even row. When working the even row, take both legs down and give them a rest. You never have to put your knitting down to make a row count!

To keep the edges as neat as possible, use a bar increase (K1f&b or P1f&b as needed, pages 22 and 88) that is nice and tight, leaving no holes, and make this increase directly in the first stitch and in the second-to-last stitch. This leaves a continuous stitch at the selvage for seaming and places the new stitch in the same spot along both edges.

Once the desired width has been reached and you have begun to decrease at one side, you can work the shaping actions on every right-side row only, which is easier to keep track of. Because this shaping will be done for only a short distance (most pieces are not much longer than they are wide), it won't throw the corners off square. Once you begin the decreasing, return to the above formula, substituting decrease for increase.

When working decreases, you may do them on the 2 edge stitches, or you may work a selvage stitch and work the decrease on the next 2 inside stitches, which will give you a neat, clean edge for seaming. Work an SSK at the beginning of a row and a K2tog at the end of a row to make the stitches slant in the correct direction.

Other Shaping

It is difficult to taper sleeves while knitting on the diagonal, so you will find that our patterns have sleeves that are worked in the traditional manner, either from the bottom up or picked up along the armhole and knitted down. A diagonal top lends itself to either a boatneck, which is straight across, or a V-neck, which can be easily shaped while knitting. Boatnecks are more suited to soft yarns that drape well, while a V-neck is good for any type of yarn.

Design Options

The first and most obvious design element is stripes. Big ones, little ones, or a combination of both, stripes on the bias are a strong graphic element. Stripes worked in garter stitch will appear more blended and less striped, especially if colors are worked for 1 row each. If you want a distinctly striped look in garter stitch, make sure your stripes are 4 or more rows. Stockinette stitch, which is much flatter by nature, will show even single-row stripes to advantage.

If you are willing to work a bit of intarsia (using more than one color in a row), you can achieve dynamic color blocks—on the diagonal! The angles give a mysterious "How did you do that?" look to your work—without the tears. When adding different yarns for color-block effects or when shaping a V-neck, use a split-ring marker to mark the exact point at which you added the new yarn or began a different shaping. Bias knitting tends to be fairly moveable, and this will help you match your backs and fronts exactly. If you work on circular needles, it is easy to slide the knitting to the wire and lay it flat for measuring.

Bias knitting can be started at any corner. We generally start the back at the bottom right corner and work toward the top left. If you work the front exactly as the back, the side edges will line up in a continuous, tubular mode.

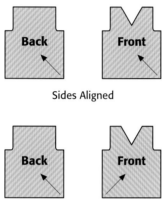

Sides Aligned

Sides Mirrored

If you work the front the reverse of the back—that is, you begin at the left bottom corner instead of the right—the side seams will line up in a chevron, and the shoulder seams will be mirrored. We generally prefer this method, as any little inconsistencies in the square of the pieces will even out more easily.

Pattern stitches look great when worked on the diagonal. If you are working an overall stitch pattern, once there are enough stitches to work a multiple, place a marker at either end of the multiple. When you have increased enough stitches for another multiple, move the markers to the outside of the new multiples, and work new stitches in pattern as you are able. An easier way is to pick a stitch pattern with no multiple, as in Lap of Luxury on page 99. Or you could break the pattern stitch with bands of plain stockinette or garter stitch. In this case, simply begin the multiple at the beginning of the row and work across to end of row, even

though the last multiple may not be a complete one as in Blue Bayou on page 90.

Yarn Suggestions

Anything goes. This is a great place to try out texture, color blocks, or color movement from corner to corner.

Fit Tips

Bias knitting drapes differently than straight knitting. In general, this style will conform to the contours of the body more readily. Make the finished measurement large enough to accommodate your largest measurement.

X **Generally flattering:** V-neck shaping is preferable to boatneck. Soft yarns will drape nicely and conform to your curves.

V **Generally flattering:** Boatneck might tend to make the shoulders appear too broad, so consider using a V-neck. Consider adding a bottom band to bring bottom edge in.

∧ **Great place for you to use stripes or pattern stitches,** particularly if worked like Blue Bayou on page 90 with a center seam and mirror-image pieces that define the V-neck. Boatnecks or V-necks are good choices. A V-neck will draw the eye upward, while a boatneck will broaden the shoulders. A shoulder gusset can be added to the top of the front and the back to open up the neck and allow a more comfortable fit, as in Brick by Brick on page 94. Consider leaving side vents at the bottom edge for ease of fit, as in Scarlet Woman on page 103.

‖ **Generally flattering:** Either neckline works. Consider going long for a tunic, dress, or coat length—you have the body style for this. Go wild!

Techniques: Beyond Getting Started

Refer to the following instructions as needed to complete your garment.

Bar Increase on Purl Side (P1f&b)

On the purl side, purl the stitch normally and don't slip it from the needle, then purl into the same stitch again, this time through the back loop, and slip the stitch from the left needle. You will notice that a purl bar appears on the right (knit) side, but don't worry; it won't really show when all is finished.

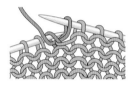
Purl into stitch but do not drop it off left needle.

Purl into back of same stitch.

Measuring

This is important in all knitting, but particularly so in diagonal work, since the gauge is not determining the finished size. You must lay the knitting flat and, without tugging at the work, measure along each edge. The 2 sides should be the same. If they are not, you may be missing some increases at one end. Work until the piece is the size needed and then begin to decrease.

Measure along side edge.

Marking

Use markers or safety pins to mark the center of the piece, for the purpose of reversing shaping to form the neck.

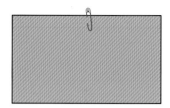
Mark the center.

Double Decrease

When you need to decrease more than one stitch at an edge, as in shaping the neck for Blue Bayou on page 90, you will use a double decrease. At the 3 stitches to be worked, slip the first stitch as if to knit, knit 2 together, and then pass the slipped stitch over the 2 stitches just worked.

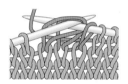
Slip 1 stitch as if to knit. Knit next 2 stitches together.

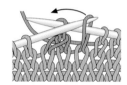
Pass slipped stitch over the knit stitch on right needle.

Color Blocks (Intarsia)

When you change yarns in the middle of a row to create color or texture blocks, as in Brick by Brick on page 94, you are working intarsia. To keep holes from appearing in the knitting, the 2 yarns must be twisted around one another. Always pick up the new yarn underneath the yarn just worked.

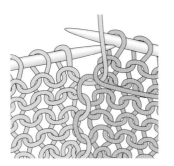

Hiding Ends

When colors are added or changed in the middle of the row, the ends must be buried in the knitting on the wrong side. To do this, thread a needle and go in and out of the purl bar on the wrong side for an inch or two. Trim, leaving a ¼" end.

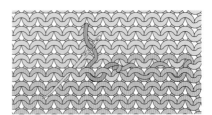

When you become more practiced, you can weave these ends in as you are knitting a row. Hold them on the back side, and move the ends up and down between each stitch, catching the ends with the working yarn.

Casual Comfort: Blue Bayou

Designed by Barry Klein

Completing this design was one of those magical moments where what you envisioned, sketched, swatched, and finished worked the entire way. *Yes!* The base yarn is Taos, which is a plied cotton that has a stonewashed look. The coordinating yarn is Flora, which is a wonderful component in colors to match Taos. To add interest to working the diagonal, I went for a textured pattern stitch that is easy to work, looks complicated, and doesn't result in a stripe. By splitting the front and back into two panels, I was able to create a V effect that adds another visual component to the sweater. This is truly one of my favorites—just add some jeans and you're ready to go.

Materials box

Size:
Small (Medium, Large, X-Large, XX-Large)

Knitted Bust Measurement:
34 (38, 42, 46, 50)"

Materials

- A 6 (7, 8, 9, 10) skeins of Trendsetter Taos (50 g, 100 yds), color 302 **3**
- B 5 (6, 6, 7, 7) skeins of Trendsetter Flora (20 g, 72 yds), color 504 (work with 2 strands throughout) **3**
- Size 7 needles or size required to obtain gauge
- Size 6 needles
- Split-ring marker
- Size F crochet hook

Gauge:
20 sts and 34 rows = 4" in garter st on size 6 needles

Yarns shown at actual size.

Waffle Stitch Pattern

Rows 1 and 2: With B, knit.

Rows 3, 5, and 7: With A, *K6, wyib sl 2, rep from *, end K6.

Rows 4, 6, and 8: With A, *P6, wyif sl 2, rep from *, end P6.

Rows 9 and 10: With B, knit.

Rows 11, 13, and 15: With A, K2, *wyib sl 2, K6, rep from *, end wyib sl 2, K2.

Rows 12, 14, and 16: With A, P2, *wyif sl 2, P6, rep from *, end wyif sl 2, P2.

Rows 17 and 18: With B, knit.

Rep rows 1–18.

Sleeves

Start with sleeves to get a feel for waffle st patt and how to make it work when new sts are added.

- With size 7 needles and 2 strands of B, CO 62 (62, 62, 70, 70) sts. Work rows 1–16 only of waffle st patt, inc 1 st at each end every 8 (6, 4, 6, 4) rows 4 (6, 8, 6, 8) times, working new sts into patt—70 (74, 78, 82, 86) sts. (Be sure to watch patt and see how waffles move and alternate so patt can be worked properly as new sts are added. If a complete rep of patt cannot be worked, work only a partial patt, but never put sl sts at edge.)
- Cont in patt until sleeve is 6 (6, 7, 7, 7)" from CO. BO all sts.
- Rep for second sleeve.

Back Panels

- **Left panel:** With size 6 needles and A, CO 3 sts. Work following stripe patt: 24 rows with A in garter st, rows 1–18 in waffle st patt, AT SAME TIME inc 1 st at each end EOR, working new sts into patt.
- When horizontal or bottom edge is 8½ (9½, 10½, 11½, 12½)" from CO point, beg new shaping. Cont in stripe patt, beg to dec at

beg of row and inc at end of row EOR until vertical edge (side edge) is 13 (13, 13½, 14, 14)" from CO point, end ready for WS row.

- Starting at side edge on WS, BO 3 (4, 4, 5, 5) sts for modified drop armhole.
- Cont in stripe patt, shaping as before until armhole vertical is 6½ (7, 7½, 8, 8½)" from BO.
- Cont in stripe patt, dec at beg and end of EOR until 3 sts remain. BO rem sts.
- **Right panel:** Work as for left panel, reversing edges of horizontal and vertical. To shape armhole, end with completed WS row and BO sts as for left panel. Note that patt will match, creating a V-shape when pieces are sewn together.

Front Panels

- Work front left panel as for back left panel until center vertical edge is 13½ (14, 15, 16, 16½)" from CO point, end ready for RS row.
- Cont in stripe patt, work double dec at neck edge (end of RS row) by working K3tog tbl EOR for a total of 8 double dec at neck edge (16 total decs). Return to regular dec at beg and end of EOR until 3 sts rem. BO.

- Make front right panel as for back right panel until center vertical edge is 13½ (14, 15, 16, 16½)" from CO point, end ready for RS row.
- Cont in stripe patt, work double dec at neck edge (beg of RS row) by working K3tog tfl EOR for a total of 8 double decs at neck edge (16 total decs). Return to regular dec at beg and end of EOR until 3 sts rem. BO.

Finishing

- Sew back panels by weaving center vertical edges tog. Rep for front panels, working up toward center V.
- Sew shoulder seams.
- Set sleeves to body by centering sleeve to shoulder seam and working down each side.
- Sew remaining underarm and side seams, tacking edge of sleeve to underarm.
- With A, work 2 rows of sc around neck edge, dec 1 st at center V by skipping a st to help shape neck. Change to B and work 1 more row of sc.
- Rep 3 rows of sc along bottom edge of front and back.

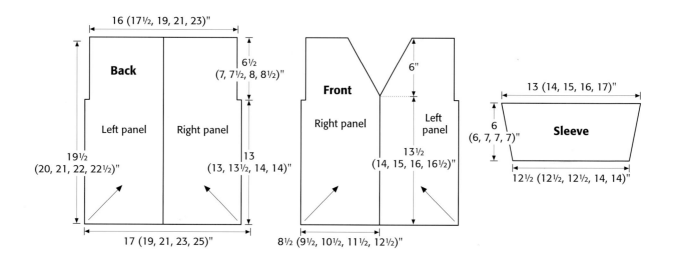

Changing the Look

Swatch A yarns: Trendsetter Taos (color 295) and Flora (color 720) are the same yarns that are used in the model sweater. The colors and textures of these 2 yarns work so well together that I had to create an additional colorway just for this wonderful sweater. See how different colors create a new look. There are actually many color combinations that will work in these 2 yarns.

Use the same quantities of yarn as the model sweater.

Swatch B yarns: Trendsetter Dolcino (50 g, 100 yds), color Red 110 and color Banana 113, and Trendsetter Sorbet (50 g, 55 yds), color M-1029

In this style of knitting, where gauge is not as important, you can play with lots of texture and color. In a whole sweater, I would have added a royal blue and a jade green to continue a complete rainbow-striped effect.

To make the sweater in these yarns, you'll need 6 (7, 8, 9, 10) skeins (divided by number of colors desired) of Dolcino and 5 (6, 6, 7, 7) skeins of Sorbet.

Yarns shown at actual size.

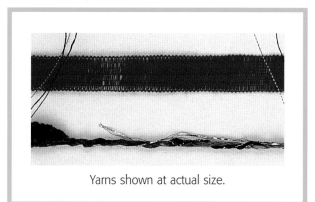

Yarns shown at actual size.

Swatch A

Swatch B

Workaday Wear: Brick by Brick

Designed by Laura Bryant

Building blocks of color create dynamic diagonals in this tee that is as fun to knit as it is to wear. The multicolored outline suggested the color selection for the bricks, with darker colors used predominantly and lighter ones appearing as occasional accents. As with all diagonal knitting, you are knitting to a measurement, not to a gauge, so it isn't critical that your gauge match exactly. That makes both substituting yarn and the final fitting of the sweater much easier. If your gauge is different, though, be aware that you may need a different amount of yarn than that specified in the pattern.

Size:
Small (Medium, Large, X-Large)

Knitted Bust Measurement:
37 (40, 43, 46)"

Materials

- **Prism Bon Bon** (2 oz, 88 yds) in the following amounts and colors:
  - **A** 2 (2, 2, 3) skeins, color 313 Blue
  - **B** 2 (2, 2, 3) skeins, color 102 Rust
  - **C** 2 (2, 2, 3) skeins, color 310 Sage
  - **D** 1 (2, 2, 2) skein, color Spice Mauve
  - **E** 1 (2, 2, 2) skein, color 314 Lavender
  - **F** 1 (2, 2, 2) skein, color 215 Coral
- **G** 4 (4, 5, 6) skeins, of Prism Luna (1 oz, 58 yds), color Harvest
- Size 7 needles or size required to obtain gauge
- Size F crochet hook
- Stitch markers

Gauge:
18 sts and 26 rows = 4" in St st with Bon Bon

Yarns shown at actual size.

Knitting the pattern: Since you are knitting to a measurement and not to a gauge, you can easily substitute yarns and needn't be concerned if your gauge doesn't exactly match ours. I have indicated how many stitches and rows for each brick in our row gauge within the pattern directions. Only work those rows if your row gauge is the same; otherwise, work the number of rows needed to get to the measurement. Work the same number of rows for each brick. If you need more width or length, you can use an extra skein of G and work gussets at the side or bottom edges as at the neck edge.

When changing yarns at the side edges, leave a long-enough tail for sewing the side seam. That way, you will have the appropriate color available for each part of the seam.

Note: Work all increases in first stitch at beginning of row and in second-to-last stitch at end of row.

Front

- With A, CO 1 st. Use bar inc (K1f&b or P1f&b) for all inc.

  Row 1: Knit, inc 1 st at each end.

  Row 2: Purl, inc 1 st at each end.

  Row 3: Knit (no shaping).

  Row 4: Rep row 2.

  Row 5: Rep row 1.

  Row 6: Purl (no shaping).

  Rep these 6 rows for 3¼ (3½, 3¾, 4)"; there should be 22 (24, 26, 28) rows.

- Work 4 rows with G. **Set up intarsia:** Cont 6-row shaping, attach B and work 10 (12, 14, 16) sts with B, drop B, attach G and work 3 sts, drop G, attach C and work rem sts in row. Work a total of 22 (24, 26, 28) rows (or same as first brick) in colors as established, twisting new yarn around yarn just worked to avoid holes.

- Work 4 rows with G. **Next row of bricks:** Work 4 sts with D, 3 sts with G, 48 (50, 52, 54) sts with E, 3 sts with G, and rem sts with B. Work as established for 22 (24, 26, 28) rows, cont incs.

- Work 4 rows with G. **Next row of bricks:** Work 34 (36, 38, 40) sts with C, 3 sts with G, 48 sts with A, 3 sts with G, and rem sts with D. Work a total of 11 (12, 13, 14) rows (or one-half of your brick count)—17 (20, 23, 26)" along either edge. Work dec as follows:

  Row 1: K1, SSK, work to last 3 sts, K2tog, K1.

  Row 2: P1, P2tog tbl, work to last 3 sts, P2tog, P1.

  Row 3: Knit (no shaping).

  Row 4: Rep row 2.

  Row 5: Rep row 1.

  Row 6: Purl (no shaping).

  Rep these 6 rows while dec.

- Work 4 rows with G. **Next row of bricks:** Work 12 (13, 14, 15) sts with F, 3 sts with G, 42 (44, 46, 48) sts with B, 3 sts with G, and rem sts with C. Work bricks as established.

- Work 4 rows with G. **Next row of bricks:** Work 30 (32, 34, 36) sts with D, 3 sts with G, and rem sts with F. Work bricks as established.

- Work 4 rows with G. **Last brick:** With E, work to last st and fasten off.

Back

Work back as for front, working rows of bricks as follows so that side seams match.

- **First brick:** With D, work half the number of rows. Work 4 rows with G, then set up next row of bricks: Work 8 (10, 12, 14) sts with C, 3 sts with G, and rem sts with A.

- Work 4 rows with G. **Next row of bricks:** Work 14 (16, 18, 20) sts with F, 3 sts with G, and rem sts with B.

- Work 4 rows with G. **Next row of bricks:** Work 3 (3, 4, 4) sts with E, 3 sts with G, 50 (54, 56, 58) sts with A, 3 sts with G, and rem sts with E.

- Work 2 rows with G, then on following 2 rows of G, beg dec as for front (your piece should match the front at the side edge). **Next row of bricks:** Work 36 (38, 40, 42) sts with D, 3 sts with G, 40 (42, 44, 46) sts with C, 3 sts with G, and rem sts with A.

- Work 4 rows with G. **Next row of bricks:** Work 38 (40, 42, 44) sts with F, 3 sts with G, and rem sts with B.

- Work 4 rows with G. Work next brick with D.

- Work 4 rows with G. Finish last brick with C.

The 2 pieces should be the same size, with side edges matching. Notice that shoulders will not match.

Shoulder Gusset

- Mark top edge of front and back 5 (6, 7, 8)" from each side edge.

- With G, PU 24 (28, 32, 36) sts along top

edge of front, from side edge to marker. Work 3 rows in St st. BO all sts loosely.

- Rep along other shoulder. Sew these gussets to back with invisible seaming.

Sleeves

- With G, on front, beg 8½ (9, 9½, 10)" from middle of shoulder gusset, PU 42 (44, 46, 48) sts to shoulder gusset seam and 42 (44, 46, 48) sts to same point on back.
- In St st, work EOR in G, with random stripes of other colors as desired (use more

of those you have more of), and dec 1 st at each edge every 4th row 8 (9, 9, 9) times— 68 (70, 74, 78) sts.

- When sleeve is 3 (3½, 4, 4½)" from PU row, work 6 rows in garter st with G. BO loosely.

Finishing

- Sew side and sleeve seams, leaving bottom brick open for side vents.
- With G, work 1 rnd sc and 1 rnd rev sc around entire bottom edge, including vents, and around neck edge.

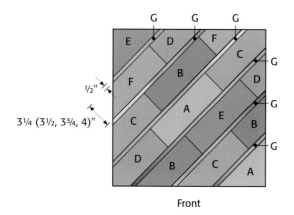

Front

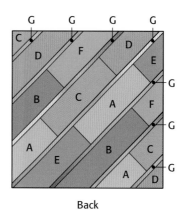

Back

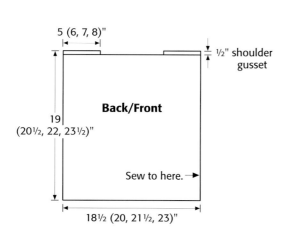

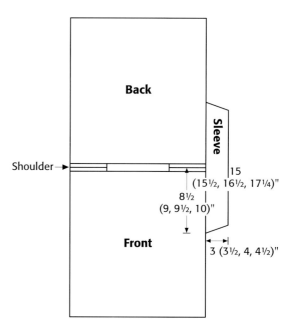

Changing the Look

Swatch A yarns: Muench String of Pearls (50 g, 99 yds), colors 4014, 4006, 4001, 4009, 4021, 4018, and Capri (50 g, 99 yds), color 14

String of Pearls comes in a great range of colors. Capri has some texture itself, but I wanted to enhance the difference even more, so I worked all of the Capri stitches in garter instead of stockinette. That causes the outlines to be raised a bit and adds another dimension. I made the bricks smaller in the swatch so that you could see all of the colors working together, but it also suggests that a smaller set of bricks would look great on the tee.

To make the sweater from these yarns, you'll need 2 (2, 2, 3) skeins of String of Pearls in each of A, B, and C; 1 (2, 2, 2) skein of String of Pearls in each of D, E, and F; and 3 (3, 4, 4) skeins of Capri.

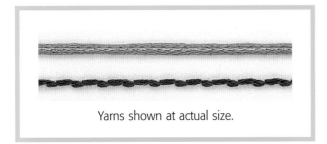

Yarns shown at actual size.

Swatch B yarns: Muench Java (50 g, 99 yds), colors 54, 46, 20, 44, and Muench Puntolinea (50 g, 99 yds), color 2

The multiple thin plies of Java impart a rustic look to this swatch. There are lots of colors to choose from, but I narrowed the choice to just 4 that I felt worked well with the multicolors in Puntolinea. The great nubby texture of Puntolinea really makes the outlines important.

To make the sweater from these yarns, you'll need a total of 9 (11, 11, 14) skeins of Java and 3 (3, 4, 4) skeins of Puntolinea.

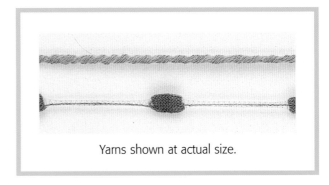

Yarns shown at actual size.

Swatch B

Swatch A

Café Chic: Lap of Luxury

Designed by Barry Klein

Checkmate—a great ribbon yarn—alternates a bright checkerboard section with a matte section. The texture in this yarn shows up best when working on a big needle in a drop-stitch pattern. Swatching really helped here, as I adjusted the needle size and changed my stitch pattern many times before getting it just right. Then came the idea of working this pattern on the diagonal. The garter wrap stitch is a little different because you work the wrap and drop stitch on the same row, which makes working increases into the pattern a bit easier. Wear this over a slip dress or a camisole—maybe even make it longer and create an incredible dress. The possibilities are endless when you're in the lap of luxury.

Size:

Petite (Small, Medium, Large, X-Large)

Knitted Bust Measurement:

34 (37, 40, 43, 46)"

Materials

- 8 (9, 10, 11, 12) skeins of Trendsetter Checkmate (50 g, 70 yds), color 811
- Size 13 needles or size required to obtain gauge
- Size 11 needles
- Size H crochet hook

Gauge:

12 sts and 12 rows = 4" in garter wrap st on size 13 needles

Yarn shown at actual size.

Garter Wrap Stitch

Row 1 (RS): Knit.

Row 2: Knit.

Row 3: Knit.

Row 4: *Insert right needle into first st on left needle as if to knit. Wrap yarn around both needles and then around just the right needle and pull the st through, removing the st from the left needle (this creates a long twisted st), rep from * across row. Watch carefully as you work this row so that your tension is even and consistent across the row.

Back and Front

- With size 13 needles, CO 3 sts. Work in garter wrap st, inc 1 st at each end of rows 1 and 3 by working the bar inc (K1f&b, page 22) in first st and second-to-last st of row. Cont in this manner, creating a triangle until horizontal or bottom edge of triangle is 17 (18½, 20, 21½, 23)" from CO point. (At this point, measurement should be same in vertical or side length as well.)
- Cont in patt, dec at beg and inc at end of rows 1 and 3 until vertical or side length is 20 (21, 22, 23, 23)" from CO point.
- Cont in patt, dec at beg and end of rows 1 and 3 until 3 sts rem. BO.
- Make second piece exactly the same.

Sleeves

- With size 11 needles, CO 36 (36, 38, 38, 40) sts. Work 3 rows in garter st.
- Change to size 13 needles and garter wrap st, inc 1 st at each end every 4 (3, 3, 3, 3) rows 3 (4, 4, 5, 5) times—42 (44, 46, 48, 50) sts. (When working an inc on a wrap row, simply work inc by making the wrap in the inc or in the new st just made.)
- Cont in patt until sleeve is 5 (6, 6, 7, 7)". BO all sts on next row 3.

Finishing

- Sew shoulder seams, leaving a center neck opening of 9".
- Set sleeves to body by centering sleeve to shoulder seam and working down each side.

- With size 11 needles, PU 50 (56, 60, 66, 70) sts evenly across bottom edge of front. Work in K1, P1 rib for 5 rows. BO in patt. Rep for bottom back edge.
- Sew underarm and side seams.
- Work 1 row of sc along open neck edge.

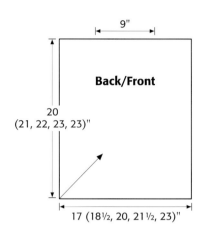

9"

Back/Front

20
(21, 22, 23, 23)"

17 (18½, 20, 21½, 23)"

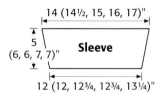

14 (14½, 15, 16, 17)"

5
(6, 6, 7, 7)"   **Sleeve**

12 (12, 12¾, 12¾, 13¼)"

Changing the Look

Swatch A yarn: Trendsetter Dolcino (50 g, 100 yds), color 108

Since this sweater is knit on the diagonal, matching gauge was not as important in picking an alternate yarn. What I was looking for was another ribbon that had lots of elasticity so that this fun drop-stitch pattern would hold, stay in place, and fit nicely to the body. Dolcino will do just that.

To make this sweater in Dolcino, you'll need 6 (6, 7, 8, 9) skeins.

Yarn shown at actual size.

Swatch A

Swatch B yarn: Prism Charmeuse (1.75 oz, 68 yds), color Orchard

This is another one of my favorite yarns because of how beautifully the yarn takes the dyes. When Laura adds color to this ribbon, it just jumps up and screams to be knit. The only thing I had to change when working with this yarn was to switch to a smaller needle because this ribbon is narrower and does not have as much elasticity. The needle change brings the stitches and the rows closer together for a perfect garment.

To make this sweater in Charmeuse, you'll need 8 (9, 10, 11, 12) skeins.

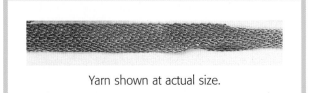

Yarn shown at actual size.

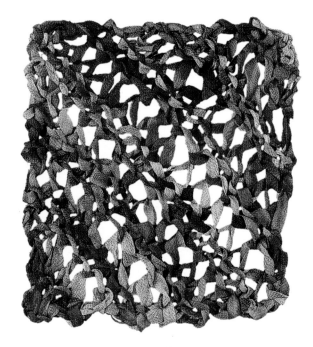

Swatch B

Glamour Girl: Scarlet Woman

Designed by Laura Bryant

Red and gold and glamour bursting out all over, this showy tee is not for the faint of heart. Wear this tee and you are sure to be noticed! A beautiful, draped rayon with gold nubs makes up the body, while Lipstick Wild Stuff, a yarn of many textures that automatically change as you knit, works its magic on a dramatic diagonal yoke. Sleeves then match the armhole edge. A V-neck follows the knitted shape naturally. Side vents are controlled with a bit of garter-stitch detail and allow ease of wearing. As dramatic as the model is, the design lends itself to many different styles of yarn: from color work, to stripes, to texture contrasted with smooth yarn. You are limited only by the scope of your imagination!

Size:

Small (Medium, Large, X-Large, XX-Large)

Knitted Bust Measurement:

36 (40, 44, 48, 52)"

Materials

- **A** 4 (5, 6, 7, 7) skeins of Prism Flash (2 oz, 125 yds), color Red **4**
- **B** 1 (1, 1, 1, 1) skein of Prism Wild Stuff (6 to 8 oz, 300 yds), color Lipstick **4**

  0 (0, 1, 1, 1) half skein of Prism Wild Stuff (3 to 4 oz, 150 yds), color Lipstick
- Size 8 needles or size required to obtain gauge
- Stitch markers
- Size F crochet hook

Gauge:

18 sts and 28 rows = 4" in St st with either yarn

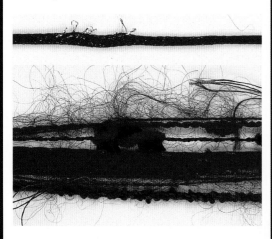

Yarns shown at actual size.

Note: Work all increases as bar increases (K1f&b or P1f&b on pages 22 and 88). Work first increase in first stitch, and second increase in second-to-last stitch.

Back

Beg at lower right corner.

- With A, CO 1 st.
- **Preparation row:** Knit into front, then back, then front of same st—3 sts.

  Row 1: Knit, inc 1 st in first st, work to last 2 sts, inc 1 st in next st, K1—5 sts.

  Row 2: Knit.

  Row 3: Knit, inc 1 st in first st, work to last 2 sts, inc 1 st in next st, K1—7 sts.

  Row 4: Knit, inc 1 st in first st, work to last 2 sts, inc 1 st in next st, K1—9 sts.

  Row 5: Knit.

  Row 6: Knit, inc 1 st in first st, work to last 2 sts, inc 1 st in next st, K1—11 sts.
- Work above rows for a total of 16 rows— bottom corner worked in garter st.
- Change rows 1, 3, and 5 to purl and cont to inc as established. Work in St st to 15¾ (17¾, 19¾, 21¾, 23¾)" or 2¼" less than desired width.

- Cont in A, but work rem 2¼" in garter st to match other corner: Work to last st of row, pm, work last st and all inc sts in garter st, keeping balance of body in St st.
- When piece is 18 (20, 22, 24, 26)" from CO point measured along edge, reverse shaping, working dec instead of inc in same rotation: on RS rows, K1, SSK at beg of row, work to last 3 sts, K2tog, K1 at end of row, or on WS rows, P1, P2tog, work to last 3 sts, p2tog tbl, P1.
- At 2¼" (end of garter-st corner), cut A and attach B. Cont to dec as established using B until 1 st rem. Fasten off.

Front

Beg at lower left corner.
- Work as for back, matching garter corners and adding B at same point on side edge.
- **Shape neck:** When dec edge is 5 (7, 8, 9, 10)", on next WS row, BO 20 (22, 24, 26, 28) sts.
- Cont to work dec at end of WS rows and beg of RS rows, but work neck edge straight for 5 (5¼, 5½, 5¾, 6)". This edge should match the bound-off sts of neck; fold front in half and check that you are ready to resume shoulder shaping.
- Return to dec at each edge. Work to 1 st, fasten off.

Sleeves

- Sew shoulder seams.
- Mark side edge 7 (7½, 8, 8½, 9)" from shoulder seam on both front and back.
- With appropriate yarn (A on A side, B on B side), PU 64 (68, 72, 76, 80) sts between markers, centering to shoulder seam.
- Work in St st, dec 1 st at each edge every 4th row 8 (9, 10, 10, 10) times—48 (50, 52, 56, 60) sts.

- When sleeve is 5 (6, 7, 8, 8½)", dec 3 sts evenly spaced across row and work 6 rows of K1, P1 rib patt. BO in patt.

Finishing

- Sew sleeve and side seams to garter corners (leave the garter st open for side slit).
- With A, work 1 rnd sc and 1 rnd rev sc around neck edge, skipping 1 st at center front to help define the V.
- With A, work 1 rnd sc and 1 rnd rev sc around bottom and side-slit edges.
- Block lightly.

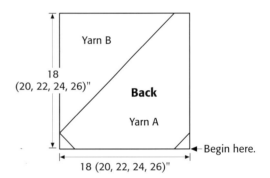

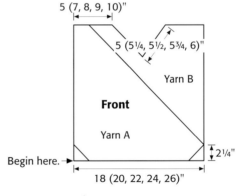

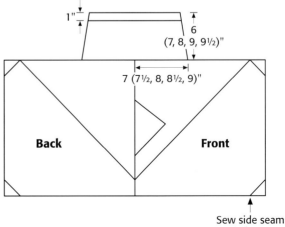

Changing the Look

Swatch A yarns: Muench String of Pearls (50 g, 99 yds), color 4001, and Prism Wild Stuff (6 to 8 oz, 300 yds), color Antique

A less sparkly but equally elegant look can be attained by substituting Muench's cotton, rayon, and nylon blend, String of Pearls, for the body, but keeping the Wild Stuff accents. The gauge is the same, and the yarn has a wonderful crispness with slightly more body than Flash. The body will have less drape, and the garment will be less formfitting. The rayon and nylon provide a sheen that isn't as glitzy as the gold flecks in Flash.

To make the sweater in these yarns, you'll need 5 (7, 8, 9, 9) skeins of String of Pearls; 1 (all sizes) skein of Wild Stuff; and 0 (0, 1, 1, 1) half skein of Wild Stuff.

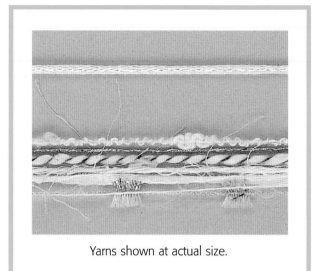

Yarns shown at actual size.

Swatch A

Swatch B yarns: Trendsetters Iguana (50 g, 82 yds), colors 851 (MC), 852 (CC)

Two multicolors of the same yarn, one with a black base and one with a white base, offset one another in more classic style. A slight texture to the yarn still produces a flatter garment whose overall impact is more tailored than glamorous and shows that even a flashy design can be tamed and tailored to suit your taste.

To make the sweater in these yarns, you'll need 6 (8, 9, 11, 11) skeins of Iguana (MC) and 3 (4, 5, 5, 5) skeins of Iguana (CC).

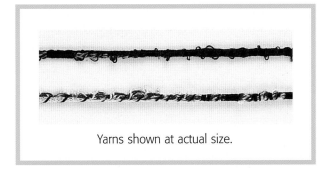

Yarns shown at actual size.

Swatch B

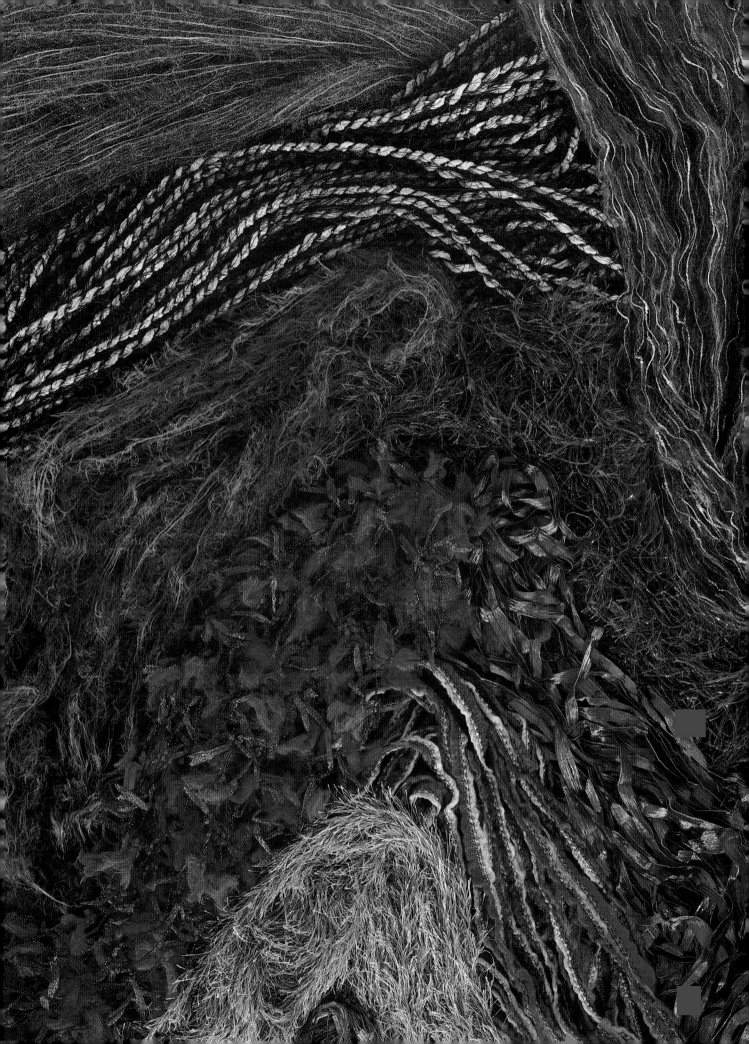

Pandora's Box

Round and round—knitting from the center out! Garter-stitch squares knit in both directions (across and sideways) give a textured, complex look to a simple technique. This unique concept works because garter stitch produces a stitch-to-row ratio that is very close to 1:2. That is, for every stitch, 2 rows are required to equal the same measurement.

Because garter stitch has a 1:2 ratio, we can work with modules that have twice the number of rows as stitches and produce very nearly a square. This is also why garter stitch uses more yarn than stockinette.

The idea is simple. Each square is worked, then without cutting the yarn, the square is rotated 90° and the next square is picked up along the edge with the same yarn. Continuing in this manner interlocks all of the squares without having to sew them together, and there are no ends to bury.

Go-rounds are ideally suited to multicolored yarns, especially if they have a long repeat of colors (as opposed to "painted" or "print" yarns, where each color appears for a short time).

Sample Squares

To learn the technique before you start a garment, work a simple sample of squares #1–#16. Refer to the diagram on page 111 as you work the squares below.

Note: Pick-up row is always considered row 1.

- **#1:** CO 8 sts and knit 16 rows. To make sure you have worked 16 full rows, count the number of ridges on each side—there will be 8. Knit across row and place sts on holder, slipping each st as if to purl. Square #1 is complete.

#2: Without cutting yarn, rotate square and PU 8 sts along side of #1 by picking up a st in every other row—in the "ditch" between garter-st ridges (see page 113), beg with the ditch after the ridge closest to holder (as opposed to ditch immediately next to holder). Knit 16 rows, then knit 1 row and place sts onto a holder as for #1. Square #2 is complete.

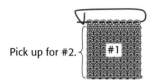

Pick up for #2.

#3: Rotate piece and PU along side of square just worked—notice that yarn is in correct place. Knit 16 rows, then knit 1 row and place sts on holder as for previous squares. Square #3 is complete.

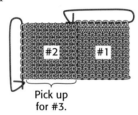

Pick up for #3.

#4: As you work this square, you must lock to edge of #1 to avoid sewing later. To do this, PU 8 sts along edge of #3, turn, and knit. Turn, knit across 7 sts, sl 1, PU in first st at edge of square you are joining to, pass slipped st over this picked-up st—beg of square is now locked to edge. Turn and knit back. Turn and knit, locking edge at end of row as above. Do this locking st at end of every RS row, and make sure you pick up a st in each st of square you are locking to. When you have finished 16 rows, knit 1 more row, place sts on holder, but don't break yarn.

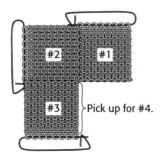

Pick up for #4.

#5: PU 8 sts along side of #1. Work 16 rows, then BO 7 sts.

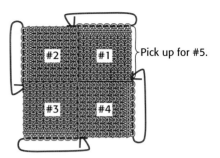

Pick up for #5.

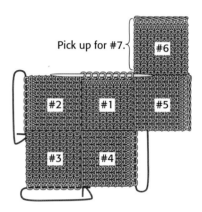

Pick up for #7.

#6: Turn, and counting st on needle as first st, PU 7 sts (8 sts on needle). Work 16 rows, then BO 7 sts.

#7: Turn, and counting st on needle as first st, PU 7 sts. As you work this square, you will have to lock again. This time locking is easier, since the sts of #1 are on a holder. Move sts from holder to third needle (a short, double-pointed needle works well). When you come to end of row 3 (counting the PU row as row 1), work SSK with 8th st of square and first st from third needle as follows: sl next st as if to knit, sl next st as if to knit, then knit those 2 sts tog through the back. Turn and work back, then rep on every RS row. Knit across onto third needle.

#8: PU 8 sts along top of #2, knit back, turn. As you work this square, you will lock to #7 at end of WS rows. Knit to last st, SSK last st with first st from third needle. Rep as established. BO 7 sts on next row.

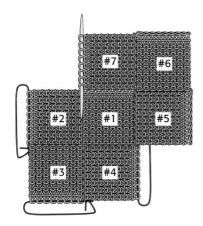

- **#9:** Turn, and counting st on needle as first st, PU 7 sts along edge of #8, knit 16 rows, then BO 7 sts on next row.

- **#10:** Turn, and counting st on needle as first st, PU 7 sts along edge of #9, knit back and turn. Move sts of #2 from holder to third needle. Work square, locking on RS to #2. Knit 1 row onto third needle.

- **#11:** PU 8 sts along edge of #3. Work square, locking on WS to #10. BO 7 sts on next row.

- **#12:** Turn, and counting st on needle as first st, PU 7 sts along edge of #11. Knit 16 rows, then BO 7 sts on next row.

- **#13:** Turn, and counting st on needle as first st, PU 7 sts along edge of #12. Move sts of #3 to third needle. Work square, locking on RS to #3, knit 1 row onto third needle.

- **#14:** PU 8 sts along edge of #4. Work square, locking on WS to #13. BO 7 sts on next row.

- **#15:** Turn, and counting st on needle as first st, PU 7 sts along edge of #14. Knit 16 rows, then BO 7 sts on next row.

- **#16:** Turn, and counting st on needle as first st, PU 7 sts along edge of #15. Move sts of #4 to third needle. Work square, locking on

RS to #4. BO 8 sts, sew top of #16 to edge of #5.

BO 7	#9	PU 7	BO 7	#8	Lock	Third needle	#7	PU 7	BO 7	#6	
				PU 8			Lock RS			PU 7	
PU 7	#10	Lock RS	Holder	#2	PU 8	Holder	#1	PU 8	#5	BO 7	
Third needle				Lock RS					Sew		
Lock WS	#11	PU 8	PU 8	#3	PU 8	Lock RS	#4	Holder	Lock RS	#16	
BO 7										PU 7	
PU 7	#12	PU 7	Lock RS	#13	Third needle	Lock WS	PU 8	#14	PU 7	#15	BO 7
	BO 7							BO 7			

Design Options

The squares can be made as large or small as you wish. Simply make sure that the number of rows is double the number of stitches. To make a sweater using the original 16 squares, decide what finished width you want and divide by 4 (there are 4 squares across). This is the measurement each square needs to be. Multiply your gauge by this measurement, and you know how many stitches your squares need to be. For example, you want the piece to be 20" wide on a gauge of 18 sts = 4". Divide 20" by 4 squares to get 5" squares. Then multiply the 5 squares times a gauge of 4½ stitches per inch to get 22.5—round this up to 23 stitches to allow for loss of width when picking up stitches. Each square will be 23 stitches by 46 rows. Remember the easy way to count rows— there will be 23 ridges on both sides of the square.

If you wish to make smaller squares, you can add as many rounds as you wish. Subsequent rounds will act just like squares #5–#16, but there will be more of them: 6 along each edge if you add 1 more round, 8 along each edge if you add 2 more rounds. To figure out how large each square needs to be, follow the same procedure as above, but divide the width measurement by 6 or 8. For example, to make a 20"-wide piece with 6 squares across, divide 20 by 6 to get 3.33; multiply that times our gauge of 4½ stitches per inch to get 14.9; round up to 15 stitches and 30 rows. To add 2 more rounds, divide the 20" by 8 to get 2.5; multiply that times 4½ stitches per inch to get 11.25; round up to 12 stitches and 24 rows.

If you are working extra rounds, don't bind off as directed above, but place subsequent edges on holders for locking until you reach the last round. Those stitches will be bound off. Half-sized squares can provide gussets and borders to bring the piece to the exact size you need.

V-necks can be calculated along the angles of the squares. Decreases worked every other row, whether worked on a horizontal or vertical square, produce a 45° angle. Neckline finishes can fill in if the neck gets too wide. Square necks are easily achieved by eliminating blocks, as is armhole shaping. Garter-stitch borders can widen a piece by becoming gussets at the underarm or can allow for neck shaping if used as a yoke, as in Party Favor on page 125. Sleeves can be plain garter stitch, which makes charting easy yet maintains continuity throughout the piece.

Another variation is to make a mitered corner square as in Tailor-Made on page 120. After completing 2 sets of 4 squares each, pick up 2 legs of a larger garter square, 1 leg on the top edge of 1 section and the other leg on the side edge of another. You then decrease these stitches in the corner, creating a larger square whose stripes change direction along the miter for a fun interplay between colors, textures, and the size of the squares.

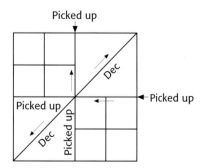

Yarn Suggestions

Alternate textured yarns with classic yarns to show them to their best advantage. Multicolored yarns and stripes show the direction of the knitting better than a single color. Stripes of highly contrasting colors make better borders than entire garments, as these stripes can become very kinetic. Since squares build one on to another, consider using different colors in different boxes. Drawing a design on paper will allow you to plan your color placement.

Fit Tips

The alternating direction of stripes makes this a flattering choice for many different figure types. Because garter stitch is thicker than stockinette, there will be extra bulk added. Thinner yarns will create less bulk; thicker yarns may become quite bulky.

X **Generally flattering.**

V **Generally flattering:** Consider using thinner yarns to reduce thickness of fabric. The bottom border can be picked up to bring in lower edge.

∧ **Generally flattering:** This is best, however, when worked in closely related colors and thinner textures. Shorter length is best, and you may wish to leave side-vent openings. Eliminate blocks at armholes to bring the shoulder line in, as in Garters Go Round on page 114.

‖ **Generally flattering.**

Techniques: Beyond Getting Started

Refer to the following instructions as needed to complete your garment.

Counting Rows

To count rows in garter stitch, count the ridges. A square will have equal ridges on both sides, and 1 ridge equals 2 rows.

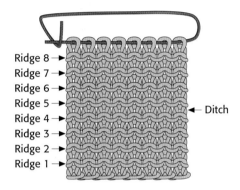

Ridge 8 →
Ridge 7 →
Ridge 6 →
Ridge 5 →
Ridge 4 →
Ridge 3 →
Ridge 2 →
Ridge 1 →

← Ditch

Picking Up Stitches in the Ditch

Pick up stitches in the ditch that is formed between 2 garter ridges.

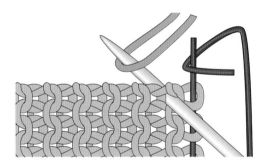

Insert needle into ditch between ridges.

Picking Up Stitches from the Wrong Side

To avoid an extra ridge on the right side of the work, the pattern will direct you to pick up stitches from the wrong side. To do this, insert the needle from the back to the front of the work as it is facing you. Wrap and draw the loop through, making the stitch. Until you get used to this, turn your work periodically to make sure that you are picking up the entire stitch; if you split a stitch, it will leave a ridge on the right side.

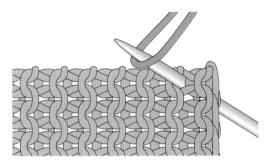

Pick up stitch from the wrong side.

Slip 1, Knit 1, Pass Slipped Stitch Over (SKP)

When locking to the side edge of an existing square or to the cast-on row, you must pick up the stitch that will be locked. Since you cannot work an SSK here, slip the last stitch of the row as if to purl, pick up a stitch in the edge of the block, then pass the slipped stitch over.

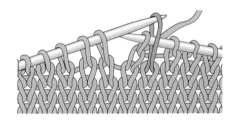

Casual Comfort: Garters Go Round

Designed by Laura Bryant

A slightly textured cotton and rayon yarn dyed in luscious landscape colors is the perfect choice for a maze of garter boxes. The entire garment is worked as the sample described in the introduction, with shaping achieved by eliminating boxes for the armholes and decreasing for the V-neck. Sizing is achieved through using boxes with different numbers of stitches. If you use a yarn with a different gauge, find out how many stitches are needed to make the right-sized square for the desired finished size, and use that number as the base number for each square. Follow the same chart for any size. It's that easy!

Note: Each size is made with the same layout of squares; however, sizing is achieved by changing the number of stitches in each square. This automatically makes the larger sizes longer, but the smaller-sized tees can be made longer by adding another row of squares at the bottom or a garter-stitch border.

Back

Remember, the PU row is always row 1.

- CO 9 (10, 11, 12, 13) sts.
- **#1:** Work garter st for 18 (20, 22, 24, 26) rows. Knit 1 row, place sts on holder.
- **#2:** Rotate square 90°, PU 9 (10, 11, 12, 13) sts along side edge (1 st per ditch). Work a total of 18 (20, 22, 24, 26) rows, knit 1 row, place sts on holder.
- **#3:** Rotate and rep as for #2.
- **#4:** Rotate and rep PU, work back. **Next row:** K8 (9, 10, 11, 12) sts, sl next st, PU 1 st in CO edge of square #1, psso. Rep PU at end of every RS row to lock #4 to edge of #1. After 18 (20, 22, 24, 26) rows, knit 1 row, place sts on holder.

Center 4 squares are complete.

- **#5:** Without breaking yarn, PU sts along edge of #1 and work as for #1.
- **#6:** PU sts along side of #5, knit 1 row, place sts on holder.
- **#7:** Move sts of #1 from holder to third needle, PU sts along edge of #6, turn and knit back, turn, K8 (9, 10, 11, 12), SSK last st with first st from #1, turn, work back. Work SSK at end of every RS row. Knit 1 row onto third needle.
- **#8:** PU sts along edge of #2, turn, K8 (9, 10, 11, 12) sts, SSK with next 2 sts, turn and knit back. Work SSK at end of every WS row. K1 row, place sts on holder.
- **#9:** PU sts along edge of #8, knit 16 rows. K1 row, place sts on holder.
- **#10:** Move sts of #2 to 3rd needle. PU sts along side of #9. Work as for #7.

- **#11:** Work as for #8.
- **#12:** Work as for #2.
- **#13:** Move sts of #3 to 3rd needle, work as for #7.
- **#14:** Work as for #8.
- **#15:** Work as for #2.
- **#16:** Move sts of #4 to 3rd needle, work as for #7. BO on last row and sew to edge of #5.

Two rounds of squares are completed—4 by 4. Cut yarn and reattach between #5 and #6.

- **#17:** PU sts along side of #6. Work as for #1.
- **#18:** Work as for #2, BO on next row.
- **#19:** Move sts of #6 to 3rd needle, work as for #7.
- **#20:** Work as for #8. BO on next row.
- **#21:** Move sts of #8 to 3rd needle, work as for #7.
- **#22:** Work as for #8. BO on next row.
- **#23:** Work as for #2.
- **#24:** Move sts of #9 to 3rd needle, work as for #7.
- **#25:** Work as for #8.
- **#26:** Move sts of #11 to 3rd needle, work as for #7.
- **#27:** Work as for #8.
- **#28:** Work as for #2. K1 row, place sts on holder.
- **#29:** Move sts of #12 to 3rd needle, work as for #7.
- **#30:** Work as for #8.
- **#31:** Move sts of #14 to 3rd needle, work as for #7.
- **#32:** Work as for #8.
- **#33:** Work as for #2. K1 row, place sts on holder.
- **#34:** Move sts of #15 to 3rd needle, work as for #7.
- **#35:** Work as for #8.
- **#36:** Move sts of #5 to 3rd needle, work as for #7. BO all sts, sew to side of #17.

Three rounds of squares completed—6 by 6. Reattach yarn between #25 and #26.

- **#37:** Work as for #2. BO on next row.
- **#38:** Move sts of #27 to 3rd needle, work as for #7.
- **#39:** Work as for #8. BO on next row.
- **#40:** Work as for #2. BO on next row.
- **#41:** Move sts of #28 to 3rd needle, work as for #7.
- **#42:** Work as for #8. BO on next row.
- **#43:** Move sts of #30 to 3rd needle, work as for #7.
- **#44:** Work as for #8. BO on next row.
- **#45:** Move sts of #32 to 3rd needle, work as for #7.
- **#46:** Work as for #8. BO on next row.
- **#47:** Work as for #2. BO on next row.
- **#48:** Move sts of #33 to 3rd needle, work as for #7.
- **#49:** Work as for #8. BO on next row.
- **#50:** Move sts of #35 to 3rd needle, work as for #7. Place sts on holder.

Back is complete.

Front

- Work as for back to square #7, then **shape neck:** Work as established for 8 (10, 10, 12, 12) rows—4 (5, 6, 6, 7) sts left from #2. BO 2 sts at beg of next 3 (5, 6, 6, 5) RS rows, BO 3 (0, 0, 0, 3) sts in last row.
- **#8:** PU as established, then dec 1 st every 4th row 5 (5, 6, 6, 7) times. Work rem sts on holder.
- Work squares #9–#19 as for back.
- **#20:** PU 4 (5, 5, 6, 6) sts along edge of #7, dec 1 st every 4th row 4 (5, 5, 6, 6) times. Fasten off.
- **#21:** Cable CO 9 (10, 11, 12, 13) sts. Use short-row shaping to **shape neck:** Knit 1 row, move sts of #8 from holder to third needle, K2 from #21, turn, K1, SSK with first st of #8, turn, K4, turn, K3, SSK with next st of #8, turn, K6, turn and cont to

work SSK as established; work 2 more sts on each WS row until all sts are used—V-neck formed.

- Work squares #22–#50 as for back.
- Sew shoulder seams.

Sleeves

- With RS facing, on left front, beg at point A, PU 54 (60, 66, 72, 78) sts to point B, knitting across sts from holders and PU 1 st in each ditch as in body. Work in garter st as follows:
  Slip sts of #50 to 3rd needle.
  Next row: Knit to last st, work SSK tog with first st from square #50.
  Next row: Knit to last st, sl 1, PU 1 st in first ditch of square #37, psso.
- Work last 2 rows until sleeve is even with side seam and all sts are used from side squares.
- Cont in garter st, dec 1 st at each edge every 4th row 4 (5, 6, 6, 7) times.
- Work 4 rows even. BO all sts loosely.
- Rep for 2nd sleeve.

Finishing

- Sew side and sleeve seams, leaving bottom square open for side vent.
- Work 1 rnd sc and 1 rnd rev sc around neck edge.
- Work 1 rnd sc and 1 rnd rev sc around entire bottom edge, including vents.

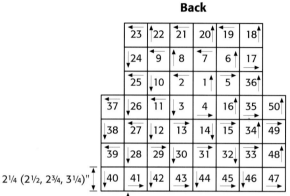

Back

2¼ (2½, 2¾, 3¼)"

↑ Indicates direction of knitting.

Front

23	22	21	20	19	18	
24	9	8	7	6	17	
25	10	2	1	5	36	
37	26	11	3	4	16	35	50
38	27	12	13	14	15	34	49
39	28	29	30	31	32	33	48
40	41	42	43	44	45	46	47

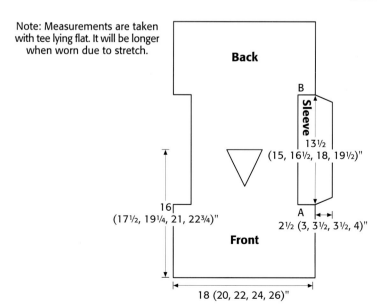

Note: Measurements are taken with tee lying flat. It will be longer when worn due to stretch.

Back

Front

Sleeve

B

13½ (15, 16½, 18, 19½)"

A

2½ (3, 3½, 3½, 4)"

16 (17½, 19¼, 21, 22¾)"

18 (20, 22, 24, 26)"

Changing the Look

Swatch A yarn: Muench Touch Me (50 g, 61 yds), color 3641

This velvety yarn must be finished, or fulled, to "set" the knit, which will keep it from forming loops, or "worms," on the surface. To full, machine wash the finished garment in warm water, then dry thoroughly in the dryer. When it comes out of the washer, it will be a small, hard ball—but the dryer softens it to an incredible velvety hand.

If you want to be very certain of your finished gauge, make the center 4 squares as we did in our swatch, then wash and dry the swatch as above and check the measurements. A 4-square swatch done on 10 stitches for each square should be 5" before fulling and 4¾" after fulling. Notice that although you can see the outlines of the squares, and there is some difference in the nap of each square, the distinctness of the garter lines is softened, and the effect will be a very soft checkerboard. Unless you are a confident knitter, this tee might be difficult to make in darker colors since the stitches could be hard to see. If you alternated two colors, as in the next swatch, the direction of the knitting would be more obvious and the stitches and rows easier to count.

To make the sweater from Touch Me, you'll need 12 (13, 17, 19, 22) skeins.

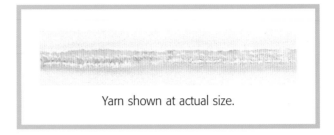

Yarn shown at actual size.

Swatch A

Swatch B yarns: Tahki Willow (50 g, 81 yds), color 845, and Stacy Charles Rondo (50 g, 88 yds), color 501

Two yarns alternated for two rows each throughout the swatch emphasize the directional knitting of the garter squares. The soft melon of Willow is repeated in the bright colors of Rondo, making the stripes of Rondo appear and disappear. Keeping the colors in the same intensity keeps the stripes from becoming too kinetic, as they might be in black and white.

To make the sweater from these yarns, you'll need 4 (5, 6, 7, 8) skeins of each yarn.

Yarns shown at actual size.

Swatch B

Workaday Wear: Tailor-Made

Designed by Barry Klein

This was the second of my two garter-stitch-square designs. I felt more secure in the process and as always, I needed to expand my knowledge and explore new ideas. My original design idea was to work the entire sweater as striped squares in Kashmir—a sexy and luscious cashmere and silk yarn. As I started knitting, I felt like I just had to add some definition to the design, so I added the large mitered squares. The look is fun yet classic. You can wear this sweater to the office, dress it up and go out to lunch with a friend, or sit next to the fire with someone you love. This sweater is tailor-made for every moment of your life.

Materials

- Trendsetter Kashmir (50 g, 110 yds) in the following amounts and colors: **3**
  - **A** 3 (3, 4) skeins, color 25628 Brown
  - **B** 3 (3, 4) skeins, color 25385 Taupe
  - **C** 3 (3, 4) skeins, color 25761 Forest Green
  - **D** 3 (3, 4) skeins, color 27018 Lime Green
- Size 8 needles or size required to obtain gauge
- Size 7 needles
- Stitch markers

Gauge:
18 sts and 36 rows = 4" in garter st on size 8 needles

Yarn shown at actual size.

Garter Square Unit A (Make 2)

- **#1 (striped square):** With size 8 needles and A, CO 20 (24, 28) sts. Knit back. Work (2 rows with B, 2 rows with A) 4 (5, 6) times, end with 2 rows with B. Then work (2 rows with C, 2 rows D) 5 (6, 7) times. BO in D on next row, leaving 1 st on needle.

- **#2 (solid square):** Rotate square #1 90°. With C, PU 1 st in first ditch below needle. Pass rem D st over new C st to turn square. Cont to PU 1 st in each rem ditch for a total of 20 (24, 28) sts. Turn and work 39 (47, 55) more rows. BO in C on next row, leaving 1 st on needle.

- **#3 (striped square):** Rotate piece 90°. With A, PU 1 st in first ditch below needle. Pass rem C st over new A st to turn square. Cont to PU 1 st in each rem ditch for a total of 20 (24, 28) sts. Turn and knit back. Work (2 rows with B, 2 rows with A) 4 (5, 6) times, end with 2 rows with B. Then work (2 rows with C, 2 rows with D) 5 (6, 7) times. BO in D on next row, leaving 1 st on needle.

- **#4 (solid square):** Rotate piece 90°. With D, PU 1 st in first ditch below needle. Pass rem D st over new D st to turn square. Cont to PU 1 st in each rem ditch for a total of 20 (24, 28) sts. PU 1 additional st by picking up CO st and knitting through it to get an extra st joining the squares. Turn. Pass second st over first st to secure squares and return to 20 (24, 28) sts. Knit back. Work 38 (46, 54) rows, joining the 2 squares by picking up next CO st and secure as before. BO all sts.

Garter Square Unit B (Make 2)

- Work striped squares #1 and #3 as in garter square unit A. For solid squares, use A for #2, and B for #4. Refer to diagram on page 123.

Front

- **Large A square:** Working with garter square unit A, turn it so stripes are vertical and striped squares are positioned in bottom right corner and top left corner. See diagram on facing page.
- With RS facing, size 8 needles, and A, PU 40 (48 56) sts, beg at bottom along right edge of garter square unit A, working into BO row of striped square and then into ditches of solid square. Position garter square unit B as shown in the diagram, pm, PU 1 st in corner, pm, PU 40 (48, 56) sts along bottom edge of garter square unit B by working into BO row of solid square and then into ditches of striped square. Knit back.
- **Work garter st in stripe patt:** Note that all PU rows equal row 1. Work 4 rows with A, 4 rows with B, 4 rows with C, 4 rows with D, AT SAME TIME dec 1 st at each side of center st EOR by working to 2 sts before center st, SSK, slip marker, K1, slip marker, K2tog, finish row. Work back even. Rep stripe patt and dec until 3 sts rem. BO.
- **Large B square:** With RS facing, PU 40 (48, 56) sts, beg at top along left edge of garter square unit B, pm, PU 1 st in corner, pm, PU 40 (48, 56) sts along top of garter square unit A. Work as for large square A until 3 sts rem. BO. Front is now complete.

Back

Position garter square units A and B as shown in diagram on facing page. Work large squares as for front, picking up sts as indicated in diagram.

Sleeves

- Sew front and back together, leaving center neck open 8 (8½, 9)".
- Mark 7½ (8, 8½)" down from shoulder seam on each side. With size 8 needles and A, PU 70 (74, 78) sts along armhole edge from marker to marker.

- **Work garter st in stripe patt:** Counting CO as 1 row, work (4 rows with A, 4 rows with B, 4 rows with C, 4 rows with D) 3 times, AT SAME TIME dec 1 st at each end every 8 rows 5 times.

- Change to size 7 needles, **work in following stripe patt:** 2 rows with A, 2 rows with B, 2 rows with C, 2 rows with D. Change to A and BO.

- Rep for 2nd sleeve.

Finishing

- With size 7 needles and A, PU 80 (92, 104) sts along front bottom edge. Knit back. **Work in following stripe patt:** 2 rows with B, 2 rows with C, 2 rows with D. Change to A and BO.

- Rep bottom stripe on back bottom edge.

- Sew underarm and side seams closed.

- **Collar:** With size 7 needles and A, PU 76 (80, 84) sts around neck edge, beg at center edge of front and working around neck edge. **Work following stripe patt:** 3 rows with A, 4 rows with B, 4 rows with C, 4 rows with D, 4 rows with A, 4 rows with B, 4 rows with C; collar should be approx 2½" wide. BO all sts in C.

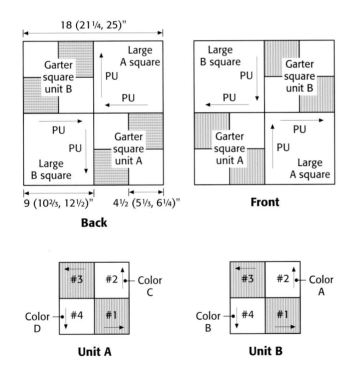

Back

Front

Unit A

Unit B

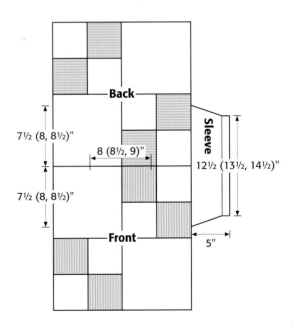

Changing the Look

Swatch A yarns:

- Lane Borgosesia Merino Otto (50 g, 120 yds), color 300 (A), color 25518 (B), color 25158 (C)
- Trendsetter Liberty (50 g, 88 yds), color 121 (D)

I selected the Merino Otto because this yarn has a wonderful twist and a great color selection. Since the Liberty has so much texture and color, I decided to play down the stripes in the alternating boxes by making each box 2 colors only (A and B; A and C).

To make this sweater with these yarns, you'll need 3 (3, 4) skeins of A and 1 (1, 2) skein each of B and C skeins in Merino Otto and 7 (8, 9) skeins of Liberty (D).

Swatch B yarns:

- Trendsetter Dune (50 g, 90 yds), color 85;
- Trendsetter Dolcino (50 g, 100 yds), color 30 Grape, color 8 Olive

After picking Dune and making my swatch, I noticed that this Dune colorway has very short colorations, making the square look like the striped square. As a result, I picked only 2 colors of Dolcino and made these my solid squares, allowing each box to have color and texture all its own.

To make the sweater from these yarns, you'll need 3 (4, 5) skeins of Dune and 3 (4, 5) skeins of each color in Dolcino.

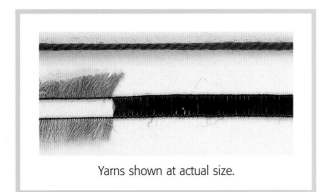

Yarns shown at actual size.

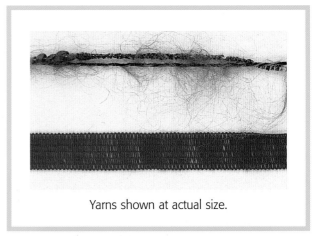

Yarns shown at actual size.

Swatch A

Swatch B

Café Chic: Party Favor

Designed by Laura Bryant

Garter boxes become the central motif on this tee that is easily sized up or down and lengthened or shortened by the gussets and borders. Neck shaping is easy because of the knitted-on yoke. You can easily customize the fit by changing the side gussets. Three different textures impart a very subtle stripe pattern to the boxes, emphasizing the directional knitting and playing textures against one another.

Size:

Small (Medium, Large, X-Large)

Knitted Bust Measurement:

36 (40, 46, 50)"

Materials

- **A** 2 (3, 4, 4) skeins of Prism Quadro (2 oz, 115 yds), color Alpine (5)
- **B** 4 (5, 5, 6) skeins of Prism Charmeuse (1¾ oz, 68 yds), color Peacock (4)
- **C** 5 (6, 7, 8) skeins of Prism Luna (1 oz, 58 yds), color Harvest (4)
- Size 11 needles or size required to obtain gauge
- Size 11 short, double-pointed needles for third needle
- 10 stitch holders
- Size G crochet hook

Gauge:

14 sts and 28 rows = 4" in garter st, alternating 1 row of each yarn

Yarns shown at actual size.

Knitting the pattern: To work 1 row of stripes with 3 yarns, cast on with A, drop A and attach B, work across with B, drop B and attach C, work across with C, drop C and A is waiting for you. To keep the yarns from snarling, place 1 on either side of you and 1 between your legs, then watch how you turn the knitting each time—one way snarls them, the other untwists them. At the end of each square, 1 yarn will have to be cut and reattached, but the same rotation of colors should be maintained.

Body (Make 2)

Note: PU row is always row 1.

- **#1:** CO 14 (15, 16, 17) sts. Work 28 (30, 32, 34) rows, using the A-B-C rotation. Knit across, place sts on holder by slipping each st as if to purl.
- **#2:** Rotate square #1 90°, then using the next yarn in rotation, PU 14 (15, 16, 17) sts in the ditches along the side of the square you just completed. Knit 28 (30, 32, 34) rows, knit across, and place sts on holder as for #1.

- **#3:** Rotate and work as for #2.
- **#4:** Rotate and rep PU as for #2, work back. Turn, knit across 13 (14, 15, 16) sts, sl 1, PU first st at edge of square #1, pass slipped st over picked-up st—st is now locked to edge. Turn and knit back. Rep locking st at end of every RS row until 28 (30, 32, 34) rows have been worked. You will be at the end of the square you are locking to. Knit across and place sts on holder, but don't break the yarn.
- **#5:** PU sts along the side of #1. Work as for #2, placing last row on holder.
- **#6:** PU sts along side of #5, work as for #2, knit across and place sts on holder.
- **#7:** PU sts along side of #6. Knit back, place sts of #1 from holder onto third needle. **Next row:** Knit to last st, SSK last st of current square and first st from #1. Turn and work back, rep SSK on every RS row. Knit across onto third needle.

- **#8:** PU sts along edge of #2, turn and knit 13 (14, 15, 16) sts, SSK last st with first st from #7. Rep as established, knit across and place sts on holder.
- **#9:** PU sts along edge of #8, work square, knit across and place sts on holder.
- **#10:** PU sts along side of #9. Place sts of #2 from holder to 3rd needle. Work as for square #7.
- **#11:** PU sts along edge of #3, work as for #8, knit across and place sts on holder.
- **#12:** PU sts along edge of #11, work as for #2, knit across and place sts on holder.
- **#13:** Place sts of #3 from holder onto 3rd needle, PU 14 (15, 16, 17) sts along edge of #12, work as for #7. Knit last row onto 3rd needle.
- **#14:** PU sts along edge of #4. Work as for #8, knit across and place sts on holder.
- **#15:** PU sts along edge of #14, work as for #2, knit across and place sts on holder.
- **#16:** Place sts of #4 from holder onto 3rd needle. Work as for #7. BO and sew top of #16 to edge of #5.

Two rounds of squares are completed, and sts on holder ready for yokes, sleeve/gussets, and bottom borders.

Front Yoke

- Start at beg of square #6, PU 56 (60, 64, 68) sts across top edge, knitting across sts from holders, and PU sts in ditch as for squares.
- Work in 3-yarn rotation, knit 3 (3, 5, 5) rows; on next row, **shape neck:** Work across 23 (24, 26, 27) sts, join 2nd ball of yarn and BO next 10 (12, 12, 14) sts, finish row. Cont in 3-yarn rotation, work each shoulder separately, and BO 3 sts at each neck edge once, BO 2 sts at each neck edge once, then dec 1 st EOR 5 (4, 4, 4) times—13 (15, 17, 18) sts on each side.
- Work to 2½ (2½, 3, 3)". BO all sts.

Back Yoke

- Work as for front to 2", then **shape neck:** Work across 18 (20, 22, 23) sts, join 2nd ball of yarn and BO 20 (20, 20, 22) sts, finish row. Cont in 3-yarn rotation, work each shoulder separately, and BO 3 sts at each neck edge once, BO 2 sts at each neck edge once—13 (15, 17, 18) sts rem on each side.
- Work to 2½ (2½, 3, 3)". BO all sts.
- Sew shoulder seams.

Side Gusset and Sleeve

- Beg at bottom corner, PU 126 (134, 144, 152) sts along side edge, working sts from holders.
- Cont 3-yarn rotation, work 1 (1½, 2½, 3)" in garter st. BO 37 (39, 42, 44) sts, work across to end, turn and BO 37 (39, 42, 44) sts—52 (56, 60, 64) sts rem for sleeves.
- Cont in 3-yarn rotation, dec 1 st at each edge every 4th row 4 (4, 5, 5) times—44 (48, 50, 54) sts.
- Work 3 more rows. BO all sts on WS.
- Rep for other side.

Bottom Border

- With A, PU 63 (70, 80, 88) sts along bottom edge, working sts from holders.
- Cont 3-yarn rotation, work ½, (1½, 2, 2½)" or to desired length. BO all sts.
- Rep for other bottom border.

Finishing

- Sew sleeve and side seam.
- With B, work 1 rnd sc and 1 rnd rev sc around neck edge.

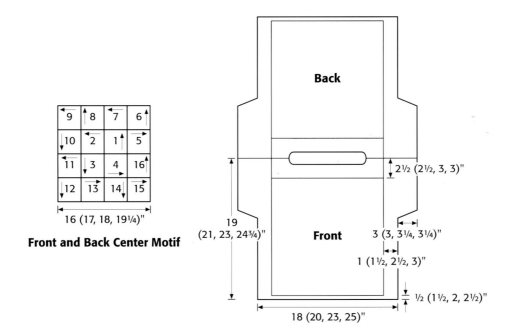

Front and Back Center Motif

Changing the Look

Swatch A yarns: Trendsetter's Zucca (50 g, 71 yds), color 5060 (A), and Prism ¼" Ribbon (2½ oz, 95 yds), color Periwinkle (B)

Soft, fluffy Zucca is alternated every 2 rows with crisp ¼"-wide rayon ribbon in a subtle multicolor, eliminating the third yarn. The look is less playful and the stripes are more distinct, but the closely related colors keep the combination from being too kinetic. Alternating the textures adds more body to ultrasoft Zucca and keeps the ribbon from becoming too stiff.

To make the sweater from these yarns, you'll need 6 (7, 8, 10) skeins of Zucca and 4 (5, 6, 7) skeins of Ribbon.

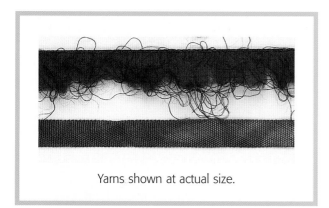

Yarns shown at actual size.

Swatch A

Swatch B yarns: Muench Davos (50 g, 95 yds), color 12 (A); Muench Puntolinea (50 g, 99 yds), color 02 (B); and Trendsetter Dolcino (50 g, 100 yds), color 8 (C)

Furry Davos, bumpy Puntolinea, and smooth Dolcino team up for a reprise of the textures in the model. A bit softer looking, with more dimension to the stitches, the feel is a nice variation without being drastically different.

To make the sweater from these yarns, you'll need 3 (4, 5, 5) skeins of Davos; 3 (4, 4, 5) balls of Puntolinea; and 3 (4, 4, 5) skeins of Dolcino.

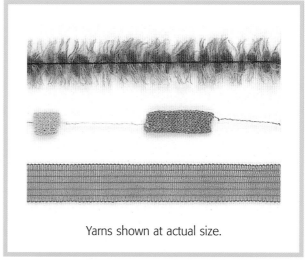

Yarns shown at actual size.

Swatch B

Glamour Girl: Domino Effect

Designed by Barry Klein

Being relatively new to knitting attached squares, my biggest challenge in this section was the design process. I thought about how I could use the boxes as an accent without having to knit them for the entire tee, making it easier for those of us who are new to this style of knitting. I cast on and started working, making medium squares. Once a four-square unit was complete, I decided to continue the checkerboard, creating the center panel. Wanting to add texture and drama to the squares, I added a touch of glitter by putting some wonderful buttons down the center to give the look of a jacket without a split front. I thought about what to do with the rest of the body and went looking for a textured yarn that would be elegant yet not overwhelming. Out came the needles and, picking up Liberty, I was set free to design the rest of the sweater. With color, texture, and detail, you are the glamour girl now.

Size:
Petite (Small, Medium, Large)

Knitted Bust Measurement:
34 (38, 42, 46)"

Materials

- **MC** 7 (8, 9, 10) skeins of Trendsetter Liberty (50 g, 80 yds), color 118 **5**

- **A** 2 (2, 2, 2) skeins of Trendsetter Sunshine (50 g, 95 yds), color 39 Linen **3**

- **B** 2 (2, 2, 2) skeins of Trendsetter Sunshine, color 13 Charcoal **3**

- Size 11 needles or size required to obtain gauge
- Size 7 needles
- Size F crochet hook
- 4 (4, 3, 3) buttons (optional)

Gauge:
14 sts and 18 rows = 4" in St st with Liberty on size 11 needles

20 sts and 36 rows = 4" in garter st with Sunshine on size 7 needles

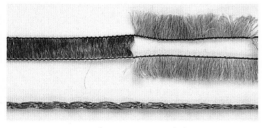

Yarns shown at actual size.

Center Panel

The units in the center panel are called boxes instead of squares because the Sunshine yarn knits up a little differently than other yarns. The garter rows yield a unit that is a bit taller than it is wide.

Note: PU row is always row 1.

- **#1:** With size 7 needles and A, CO 15 (15, 17, 17) sts. Work in garter st for 30 (30, 34, 34) rows. BO on next row, leaving 1 st on needle.

- **#2:** Join B and *PU 1 st in ditch between garter-st ridges, pass A st over B st. Cont to PU 1 st in each ditch for a total of 15 (15, 17, 17) sts. Work in garter st for 30 (30, 34, 34) rows. BO on next row, leaving 1 st on needle.*

- **#3:** Join A and rep from * to *, passing B st over A st.

- **#4:** Join B and PU 1 st in ditch, pass A st over B st. Cont to PU 1 st in each ditch for a total of 15 (15, 17, 17) sts. PU 1 additional st in CO row of first square. Turn work and pass second st over first st to lock boxes and get back to original number of sts. Work back. Work final box in garter st, locking to original box as above on EOR for a total of 30 (30, 34, 34) rows. BO.

- Follow diagram on page 132, adding boxes #5–#10 to complete center panel, picking up sts and locking squares as necessary, and keeping checkerboard: work #5–#8 separately as for #1–#4, then sew edge of #7 to edge of #2 and edge of #8 to edge of #1.

- **#9:** PU along #4, BO at end.

- **#10:** PU along #9, lock to #3 on WS.

Front Panels (Make 2)

- With size 11 needles and MC, CO 20 (22, 24, 28) sts. Work in St st to 13 (14, 14, 15)" from beg.
- **Shape armhole:** BO 3 (4, 5, 6) sts at beg of next RS row to create armhole, dec 1 st at beg of next 4 (5, 6, 8) RS rows—13 (13, 13, 14) sts. Cont until panel is 17½ (17½, 19, 19)" from beg.
- **Shape neck:** Dec 1 st at neck edge EOR 2 (2, 2, 3) times. Cont until panel is 19½ (21, 21½, 23)" from beg. BO all sts.
- Make another panel, reversing shaping by starting armhole shaping on purl row or WS row at desired length. Finish balance of front to mirror image.

Back

- With size 11 needles and MC, CO 61 (65, 72, 80) sts. Work in St st to 13 (14, 14, 15)" from beg.
- **Shape armhole:** BO 3 (4, 5, 6) sts at beg of next 2 rows, dec 1 st at each end EOR 4 (5, 6, 8) times—47 (47, 50, 52) sts. Cont until armhole is 6½ (7, 7½, 8)". BO all sts.

Sleeves

- With size 7 needles and A, CO 6 sts. Work in garter st for 12 rows.

- Work alternating checkerboard boxes like center panel, working boxes of 6 sts by 12 rows until strip is 10 (10, 12, 12)" long.
- With size 11 needles and MC, PU 33 (33, 35, 35) sts along edge of checkerboard strip. Work in St st, inc 1 st at each end EOR 7 (8, 8, 9) times—47 (49, 51, 53) sts on needle.
- Cont until sleeve is 6 (6, 7, 7)" from beg, including checkerboard band.
- BO 3 (4, 5, 6) sts at beg of next 2 rows, dec 1 st at each end EOR until cap is 4 (4½, 5, 5½)".
- BO 2 sts at beg of next 2 rows. BO rem sts.

Finishing

- Pin and sew center panel between 2 side panels, from CO edge to neck shaping.
- Sew shoulder seams.
- Set sleeves to body by centering cap to shoulder seam and working down each side.
- Sew remaining underarm and side seams closed.
- With B, work 1 row of sc around neck edge, back neck, and opposite neck edge. Change to A and work 1 row of rev sc around same areas; cont across fronts, matching colors.
- With A, work 1 row of sc and 1 row rev sc along bottom edge of MC; match colors along front checkerboard boxes to finish off on each row.
- Sew buttons in center of intersecting checkerboard boxes on front if desired.

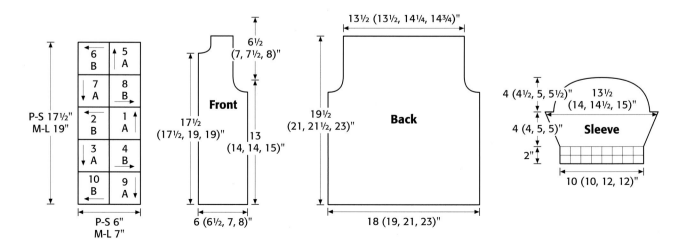

Changing the Look ▪ ▪ ▪

Swatch A yarns: Trendsetter Aura (50 g, 148 yds), color 7502 (A), color 3185 (B), and Trendsetter Chic (50 g, 55 yds), color 57

Since this design is for the glamour girl, I went for even more sparkle by using Aura for the center checkerboard. Aura has a hint of glimmer and is fun to knit. Chic is used for the body and is worked in reverse stockinette stitch to allow the colors and texture to show.

To make the sweater from these yarns, you'll need 1 (1, 1, 1) skein each of A and B in Aura and 10 (12, 14, 16) skeins of Chic.

Swatch B yarns: Trendsetter Spiral (50 g, 110 yds), color 103 (A), color 96 (B), and Trendsetter Dune (50 g, 90 yds), color 96

Spiral is a ribbon yarn with bright rayon patches that add subtle texture to the checkerboard squares. The side panels are made with the ultimate of knitting yarns, Dune, which adds the glamour and glitz.

To make the sweater from these yarns, you'll need 2 (2, 2, 2) skeins of each color in Spiral and 7 (8, 9, 10) skeins of Dune.

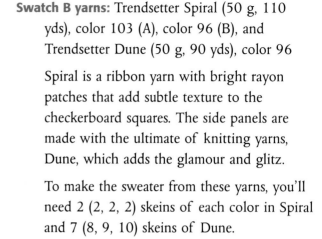

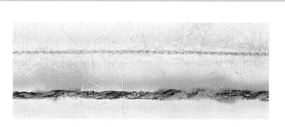

Yarns shown at actual size.

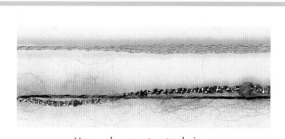

Yarns shown at actual size.

Swatch A

Swatch B

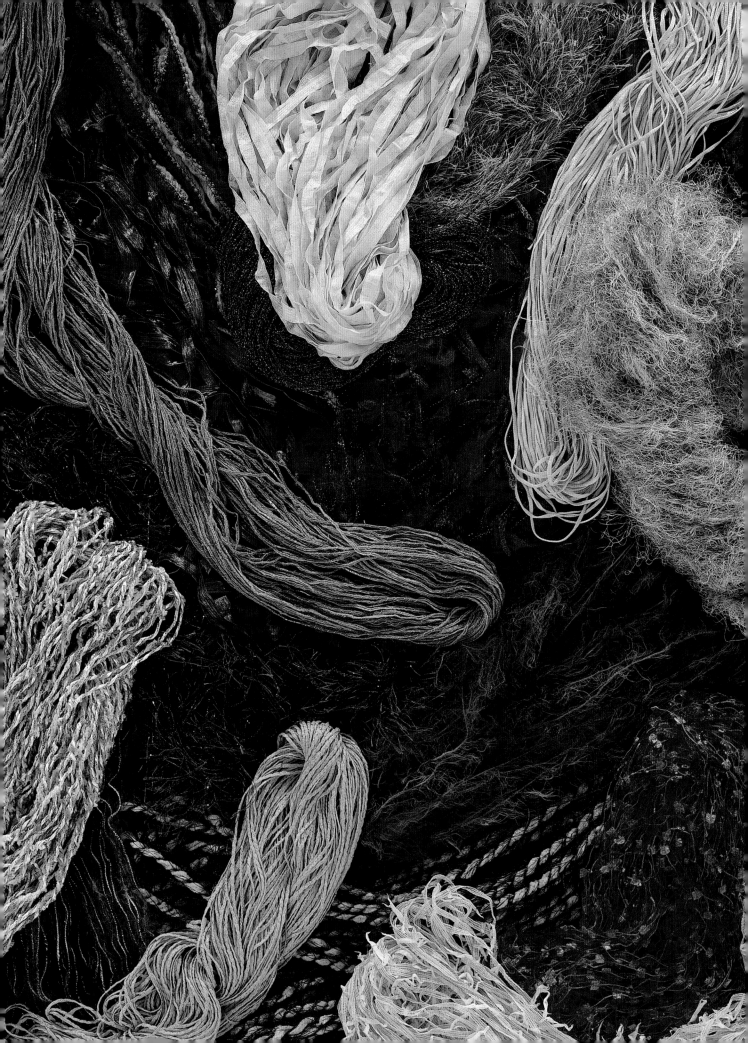

Wrapping It Up

Once everything is knit, the really fun part begins—you are almost there! Putting the pieces together can "seam" like a daunting task. You have gained new techniques for knitting; now learning how to finish your sweater will also make you a better knitter. Keep your gauge swatches and practice the techniques below. We recommend that you play with these swatches and not your garment; you will gain confidence as you practice. Many local yarn stores, guilds, and consumer shows offer classes on finishing. If you still feel like you need some extra help, sign up and learn more at the hands of an expert.

We recommend gently blocking each piece with steam after knitting. You can use an ironing board, a bed, or an out-of-the-way section of carpet covered with a sheet. Use T-pins to keep the pieces flat and to size while you steam. Refer to the diagram as a guide for laying out the pieces, wrong side up. With a steamer (our favorite is a Jiffy tank steamer with hose, but a small Jiffy or other travel steamer or even a good steam iron, such as a Rowenta, will work), gently steam the entire surface, paying particular attention to any edges that might be rolling. Be careful not to put the weight of the iron on the pieces. Allow the knitting to dry; then remove the pins and you are ready for seaming.

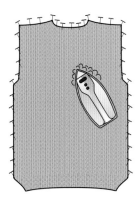

Seams

The method for seaming depends on the type of seams that you are joining. We've listed our favorite methods below.

Shoulder Seams

For shoulder seams, we bind off firmly, then weave the seams together on the right side. This provides an almost invisible seam. By binding off firmly rather than loosely, you have provided stability for the shoulder area. You can also pull the seam tighter to provide more stability on heavier yarns.

Place the 2 pieces on a table, right sides up and shoulders aligned. With yarn attached, insert the needle into the V of the first stitch on the piece nearest you, then through the V of the first stitch on the other piece. Insert the needle through both threads that make the V of the next stitch on the piece nearest you, then through the threads of the same V on the other piece. Pull the tension just enough so that the stitch you have made looks just like the knitting.

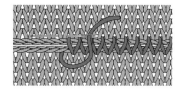

Vertical Seams

Our preferred method for sewing vertical seams is the mattress stitch, which is worked from the right side and provides an invisible seam. Some knitters like to add 2 stitches to the pattern to provide for a full stitch being lost at the seams. *All the patterns in this book include edge stitches.*

The mattress stitch is worked from the right side of the knitting. Place the 2 pieces on a table, right side up and aligned along the edge to be sewn. Begin at the lower edge, either with the long tail from the cast on or with new yarn attached firmly to the selvage. Insert the needle under 2 horizontal bars between the first and second stitches from the edge, then under 2 stitches at the same place on the opposite piece. Pull the yarn firmly in the direction of the open portion of the seam. Be sure to go into the stitch you came out of and then proceed up, working under 2 horizontal bars on each side and pulling the seam together as you work. The most common mistake is when you don't "go in where you came out."

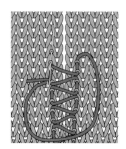

Pull tight every inch or so.

Other Seams

To sew set-in, inset, or drop-shouldered sleeves to the body, use the mattress stitch along the sides of the sleeve and combine it with invisible weaving along the body piece where the cap levels off at the top. Set the sleeve top or sleeve cap to the body by centering it to the shoulder seam and working down each side separately.

Edgings

Each project specifies the type of edge finish we think works best. Most are simple rib or garter-stitch edges, and some are picked up and worked after knitting. One edge we use often is a row of single crochet followed by a row of reverse single crochet (also known as crab stitch) or slip stitch. This can be worked successfully on pieces that have little natural roll.

Single Crochet

Working from right to left with the right side of the work facing you, insert a crochet hook into the first knit stitch, draw up a loop, wrap yarn around the hook, and draw it through the loop on the hook (yarn fastened to knitting); *insert the hook into the next stitch, draw up a loop, wrap the yarn around the hook, and draw through both loops (stitch made)*; repeat from * to *.

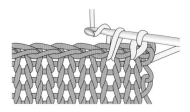

Insert hook into stitch, yarn over hook, pull loop through to front, yarn over hook.

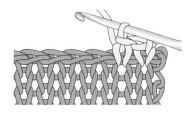

Pull loop through both loops on hook.

For correct spacing, work 1 stitch in each knit stitch for 3 or 4 stitches, then skip 1; on row edges, work 1 stitch for 2 rows, then skip 1 row. Crochet takes up more room than knitting, and if you work 1 stitch in each stitch, your edge will be too crowded with stitches and will ruffle. Once you begin the crochet, stop every few inches and look at the edge. It should be just barely tighter than the knitting, since the row of reverse crochet will spread it out a bit more.

Reverse Single Crochet

This stitch is usually worked on a foundation row of single crochet. Working from left to right, with right side facing, insert the hook into the single crochet stitch to the right, draw up a loop, then wrap and draw through both loops (stitch made). Repeat, moving from left to right.

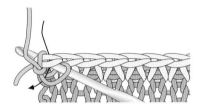

Join yarn with slip stitch. Insert hook into first stitch to the right.

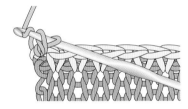

Yarn over hook, pull through both loops on hook, keeping hook parallel to work.

Always keep your hook parallel to the work. If you twist your hand around when inserting the hook, the stitch will be incorrect. Notice that keeping your hook parallel to the work is a bit awkward, but it gets easier as you practice. Keeping the tension a bit looser makes it easier to work.

Slip Stitch

This must be worked on a foundation row of single crochet. Working in the same direction as single crochet, insert the hook into the single crochet stitch, *draw up a loop and pull this new loop through the existing loop on the hook. Insert the hook into the next stitch, repeat from * across the row. Watch the tension carefully to keep it even and consistent across the row.

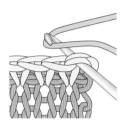

Insert hook under both loops of stitch. Yarn over hook.

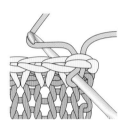

Insert hook under both loops of stitch. Yarn over hook.

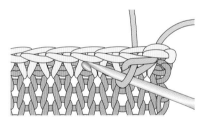

Pull loop of yarn through stitch and loop on hook.

A variation is to pick up only one-half of the single crochet stitch (half of the V) and work the slip stitch. This will push the remaining half of the V toward the front and create a nice ridge stitch.

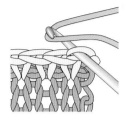 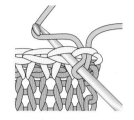

Insert hook under back loop of stitch. Yarn over hook.   Insert hook under back loop of stitch. Yarn over hook.

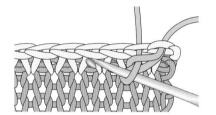

Pull loop of yarn through stitch and loop on hook.

Final Finishing

The final touch should be another session with your steamer. With the garment inside out, gently pat the steam onto all seams to flatten them slightly. Pat the neck and front bands and allow the garment to dry. Voilà!—your knitting is ready to wear!

Care

Most knitted garments can be gently hand washed in mild detergent and lukewarm water. Yarn labels that say "dry clean only" should be followed, but if a label reads "dry cleaning recommended," gentle hand washing should not harm the fibers.

The key to washing any fine textile is to neither shock nor stretch it. Shocking occurs when the water temperature is varied by more than a few degrees. Stretching occurs through agitation or by picking up a heavy, wet garment by one part or edge. The wash and rinse waters should be the same temperature, and the entire garment must be supported as it is lifted from the basin. The wet garment can be placed in the washing machine and run through the "spin" cycle to help remove excess water. The garment can be placed in a lingerie bag to provide extra protection. Be certain that the washer is set on spin only, with no agitation and no rinse water coming in. Remove the garment and lay it flat on a screen or towel, patting it into shape. Allow to dry. The surface may be brushed gently with a lint brush to raise the nap.

Knitting Abbreviations

approx	approximately
beg	begin, beginning
BO	bind off
CC	contrasting color
cn	cable needle
CO	cast on
cont	continue
dec	decrease(s), decreasing
EOR	every other row
g	grams
garter st	garter stitch—back and forth: knit every row; in the round: knit one round, purl one round
inc	increase(s), increasing
K	knit
K1f&b	bar increase on knit side—knit into front and back of same stitch (page 22)
K2tog	insert needle into 2 stitches and knit together (page 23)
K3tog tbl	insert needle into 3 stitches and knit together through the back loops
K3tog tfl	insert needle into 3 stitches and knit together through the front loops
MC	main color
oz	ounces
P	purl
P2tog	insert needle into 2 stitches and purl together
P2tog tbl	insert needle into 2 stitches through the back loops and purl together
P1f&b	bar increase on purl side—purl into front and back of same stitch (page 88)

patt	pattern
pm	place marker
psso	pass slipped stitch over
PU	pick up
rem	remain(s), remaining
rep	repeat(s)
rev sc	reverse single crochet (page 137)
rev St st	reverse stockinette stitch—back and forth: purl right-side rows, knit wrong-side rows; in the round: purl every row
rib	any combination of knits and purls that line up row after row: For example, K1, P1 every row, K2, P2 every row, and so on.
rnd(s)	round(s)
RS	right side
sc	single crochet (page 136)
sl	slip stitch from left to right needle as if to purl unless specified otherwise
SKP	slip 1 stitch as if to knit, knit 1, pass slipped stitch over (page 113)
SSK	slip 1 stitch as if to knit, slip another stitch as if to knit, knit these 2 stitches together (page 23)
st(s)	stitch(es)
St st	stockinette stitch—back and forth: knit right-side rows, purl wrong-side rows; in the round: knit every round
tog	together
wyib	with yarn in back
wyif	with yarn in front
WS	wrong side
yds	yards
YO	yarn over needle

Yarn Conversion Chart

Yards	x .91	= meters
Meters	x 1.09	= yards
Grams	x .0352	= ounces
Ounces	x 28.35	= grams

Yarn-Weight Symbols and Categories

Yarn-Weight Symbol & Category Names	1 SUPER FINE	2 FINE	3 LIGHT	4 MEDIUM	5 BULKY	6 SUPER BULKY
Types of Yarns in Category	Sock, Fingering, Baby	Sport, Baby	DK, Light Worsted	Worsted, Afghan, Aran	Chunky, Craft, Rug	Bulky, Roving
Knit Gauge Ranges in Stockinette Stitch to 4"	27 to 32 sts	23 to 26 sts	21 to 24 sts	16 to 20 sts	12 to 15 sts	6 to 11 sts
Recommended Needle in US Size Range	1 to 3	3 to 5	5 to7	7 to 9	9 to 11	11 and larger

Suggested Reading List

The Knitter's Companion by Vicki Square. Published in 1996 by Interweave Press, Inc.: Loveland, Colorado.

A Knitter's Template by Laura Militzer Bryant and Barry Klein. Published in 2002 by Martingale & Company: Woodinville, Washington.

Knitting with Novelty Yarns by Laura Militzer Bryant and Barry Klein. Published in 2001 by Martingale & Company: Woodinville, Washington.

Vogue Knitting. Published in 2002 by Sixth and Spring Books: New York.

Resources

For a list of shops in your area or mail-order/Internet companies that carry the yarns mentioned in this book, write to the following companies or visit their Web sites:

Lana Borgosesia
16745 Saticoy St. #101
Van Nuys, CA 91406
www.trendsetteryarns.com

Muench Yarns
285 Bel Marin Keys Blvd.
Novato, CA 94949
www.muenchyarns.com

Prism
3140 39th Ave. N
St. Petersburg, FL 33714
www.prismyarn.com

Tahki/Stacy Charles Inc.
8000 Cooper Avenue Bldg. 6
Glendale, NY 11385-7734
www.tahkistacycharles.com

Trendsetter
16745 Saticoy St. #101
Van Nuys, CA 91406
www.trendsetteryarns.com

New and Bestselling Titles from

Martingale®
& C O M P A N Y

America's Best-Loved Craft & Hobby Books®
America's Best-Loved Knitting Books®

That Patchwork Place®

America's Best-Loved Quilt Books®

NEW RELEASES
300 Paper-Pieced Quilt Blocks
American Doll Quilts
Classic Crocheted Vests
Dazzling Knits
Follow-the-Line Quilting Designs
Growing Up with Quilts
Hooked on Triangles
Knitting with Hand-Dyed Yarns
Lavish Lace
Layer by Layer
Lickety-Split Quilts
Magic of Quiltmaking, The
More Nickel Quilts
More Reversible Quilts
No-Sweat Flannel Quilts
One-of-a-Kind Quilt Labels
Patchwork Showcase
Pieced to Fit
Pillow Party!
Pursenalities
Quilter's Bounty
Quilting with My Sister
Seasonal Quilts Using Quick Bias
Two-Block Appliqué Quilts
Ultimate Knitted Tee, The
Vintage Workshop, The
WOW! Wool-on-Wool Folk-Art Quilts

KNITTING
Basically Brilliant Knits
Beyond Wool
Classic Knitted Vests
Comforts of Home
Dazzling Knits **NEW!**
Fair Isle Sweaters Simplified
Garden Stroll, A
Knit it Now!
Knits for Children and Their Teddies
Knits from the Heart
Knitted Shawls, Stoles, and Scarves
Knitted Throws and More
Knitter's Book of Finishing Techniques, The
Knitter's Template, A
Knitting with Hand-Dyed Yarns **NEW!**
Knitting with Novelty Yarns
Lavish Lace **NEW!**
Little Box of Scarves, The
Little Box of Sweaters, The
More Paintbox Knits

Pursenalities **NEW!**
Simply Beautiful Sweaters
Simply Beautiful Sweaters for Men
Style at Large
Too Cute!
Treasury of Rowan Knits, A
Ultimate Knitted Tee, The **NEW!**
Ultimate Knitter's Guide, The

CROCHET
Classic Crocheted Vests **NEW!**
Crochet for Babies and Toddlers
Crochet for Tots
Crocheted Aran Sweaters
Crocheted Lace
Crocheted Socks!
Crocheted Sweaters
Today's Crochet

CRAFTS
20 Decorated Baskets
Beaded Elegance
Blissful Bath, The
Collage Cards
Creating with Paint
Holidays at Home
Pretty and Posh
Purely Primitive
Stamp in Color
Trashformations
Warm Up to Wool
Year of Cats…in Hats!, A

APPLIQUÉ
Appliquilt in the Cabin
Blossoms in Winter
Garden Party
Shadow Appliqué
Stitch and Split Appliqué
Sunbonnet Sue All through the Year

LEARNING TO QUILT
101 Fabulous Rotary-Cut Quilts
Happy Endings, Revised Edition
Loving Stitches, Revised Edition
More Fat Quarter Quilts
Quilter's Quick Reference Guide, The
Sensational Settings, Revised Edition
Simple Joys of Quilting, The
Your First Quilt Book (or it should be!)

PAPER PIECING
40 Bright and Bold Paper-Pieced Blocks
50 Fabulous Paper-Pieced Stars
Down in the Valley
Easy Machine Paper Piecing
For the Birds
Papers for Foundation Piecing
Quilter's Ark, A
Show Me How to Paper Piece
Traditional Quilts to Paper Piece

QUILTS FOR BABIES & CHILDREN
Easy Paper-Pieced Baby Quilts
Easy Paper-Pieced Miniatures
Even More Quilts for Baby
More Quilts for Baby
Quilts for Baby
Sweet and Simple Baby Quilts

ROTARY CUTTING/SPEED PIECING
365 Quilt Blocks a Year Perpetual
   Calendar
1000 Great Quilt Blocks
Burgoyne Surrounded
Clever Quarters
Clever Quilts Encore
Endless Stars
Once More around the Block
Pairing Up
Stack a New Deck
Star-Studded Quilts
Strips and Strings
Triangle-Free Quilts

Our books are available at
bookstores and your favorite
craft, fabric, and yarn retailers.
If you don't see the title
you're looking for, visit us at
www.martingale-pub.com
or contact us at:

1-800-426-3126

International: 1-425-483-3313
Fax: 1-425-486-7596
Email: info@martingale-pub.com